THE PELICAN SHAKESPEARE
GENERAL EDITORS

STEPHEN ORGEL
A. R. BRAUNMULLER

The Merchant of Venice

Ellen Terry as Portia in the trial scene (IV.1) at the Lyceum Theatre, 1880. The Shylock was Henry Irving.

William Shakespeare

The Merchant of Venice

EDITED BY A. R. BRAUNMULLER

PENGUIN BOOKS

PENGUIN BOOKS

Published by the Penguin Group

Penguin Group (USA) Inc., 375 Hudson Street,
New York, New York 10014, U.S.A.
Penguin Group (Canada), 90 Eglinton Avenue East, Suite 700, Toronto,
Ontario, Canada M4P 2Y3 (a division of Pearson Penguin Canada Inc.)
Penguin Books Ltd, 80 Strand, London WCR2 0RL, England
Penguin Ireland, 25 St. Stephen's Green, Dublin 2, Ireland
(a division of Penguin Books Ltd)
Penguin Books Australia Ltd, 250 Camberwell Road, Camberwell,
Victoria 3124, Australia (a division of Pearson Australia Group Pty Ltd)
Penguin Books India Pvt Ltd, 11 Community Centre,
Panchsheel Park, New Delhi – 110 017, India
Penguin Group (NZ), Cnr Airborne and Rosedale Roads, Albany,
Auckland 1310, New Zealand (a division of Pearson New Zealand Ltd)
Penguin Books (South Africa) (Pty) Ltd, 24 Sturdee Avenue,
Rosebank, Johannesburg 2196, South Africa

Penguin Books Ltd, Registered Offices: 80 Strand, London
WC2R 0RL, England

The Merchant of Venice edited by Brents Stirling published in the United
States of America in Penguin Books 1959
Revised edition published 1970
This new edition edited by A. R. Braunmuller published 2000

14 16 18 20 19 17 15

Copyright © Penguin Books Inc., 1959, 1970
Copyright © Penguin Putnam Inc., 2000
All rights reserved

ISBN 0-14-07.1462 6
(CIP data available)

Printed in the United States of America
Set in Adobe Garamond
Designed by Virginia Norey

Contents

Publisher's Note

IT IS ALMOST half a century since the first volumes of the Pelican Shakespeare appeared under the general editorship of Alfred Harbage. The fact that a new edition, rather than simply a revision, has been undertaken reflects the profound changes textual and critical studies of Shakespeare have undergone in the past twenty years. For the new Pelican series, the texts of the plays and poems have been thoroughly revised in accordance with recent scholarship, and in some cases have been entirely reedited. New introductions and notes have been provided in all the volumes. But the new Shakespeare is also designed as a successor to the original series; the previous editions have been taken into account, and the advice of the previous editors has been solicited where it was feasible to do so.

Certain textual features of the new Pelican Shakespeare should be particularly noted. All lines are numbered that contain a word, phrase, or allusion explained in the glossarial notes. In addition, for convenience, every tenth line is also numbered, in italics when no annotation is indicated. The intrusive and often inaccurate place headings inserted by early editors are omitted (as is becoming standard practice), but for the convenience of those who miss them, an indication of locale now appears as the first item in the annotation of each scene.

In the interest of both elegance and utility, each speech prefix is set in a separate line when the speaker's lines are in verse, except when those words form the second half of a verse line. Thus the verse form of the speech is kept visually intact. What is printed as verse and what is printed as prose has, in general, the authority of the original texts. Departures from the original texts in this regard have only the authority of editorial tradition and the judgment of the Pelican editors; and, in a few instances, are admittedly arbitrary.

The Theatrical World

Economic realities determined the theatrical world in which Shakespeare's plays were written, performed, and received. For centuries in England, the primary theatrical tradition was nonprofessional. Craft guilds (or "mysteries") provided religious drama – mystery plays – as part of the celebration of religious and civic festivals, and schools and universities staged classical and neoclassical drama in both Latin and English as part of their curricula. In these forms, drama was established and socially acceptable. Professional theater, in contrast, existed on the margins of society. The acting companies were itinerant; playhouses could be any available space – the great halls of the aristocracy, town squares, civic halls, inn yards, fair booths, or open fields – and income was sporadic, dependent on the passing of the hat or on the bounty of local patrons. The actors, moreover, were considered little better than vagabonds, constantly in danger of arrest or expulsion.

In the late 1560s and 1570s, however, English professional theater began to gain respectability. Wealthy aristocrats fond of drama – the Lord Admiral, for example, or the Lord Chamberlain – took acting companies under their protection so that the players technically became members of their households and were no longer subject to arrest as homeless or masterless men. Permanent theaters were first built at this time as well, allowing the companies to control and charge for entry to their performances.

Shakespeare's livelihood, and the stunning artistic explosion in which he participated, depended on pragmatic and architectural effort. Professional theater requires ways to restrict access to its offerings; if it does not, and admission fees cannot be charged, the actors do not get paid, the costumes go to a pawnbroker, and there is no such thing as a professional, ongoing theatrical tradition. The answer to that economic need arrived in the late 1560s and 1570s with the creation of the so-called public or amphitheater playhouse. Recent discoveries indicate that the precursor of the Globe playhouse in London (where Shakespeare's mature plays were presented) and the Rose theater (which presented Christopher Marlowe's plays and some of Shakespeare's earliest ones) was the Red Lion theater of 1567. Archaeological studies of the foundations of the Rose and Globe theaters have revealed that the open-air theater of the 1590s and later was probably a polygonal building with fourteen to twenty or twenty-four sides, multistoried, from 75 to 100 feet in diameter, with a raised, partly covered "thrust" stage that projected into a group of standing patrons, or "groundlings," and a covered gallery, seating up to 2,500 or more (very crowded) spectators.

These theaters might have been about half full on any given day, though the audiences were larger on holidays or when a play was advertised, as old and new were, through printed playbills posted around London. The metropolitan area's late-Tudor, early-Stuart population (circa 1590-1620) has been estimated at about 150,000 to 250,000. It has been supposed that in the mid-1590s there were about 15,000 spectators per week at the public theaters; thus, as many as 10 percent of the local population went to the theater regularly. Consequently, the theaters' repertories – the plays available for this experienced and frequent audience – had to change often: in the month between September 15 and October 15, 1595, for instance, the Lord Admiral's Men performed twenty-eight times in eighteen different plays.

Since natural light illuminated the amphitheaters' stages, performances began between noon and two o'clock and ran without a break for two or three hours. They often concluded with a jig, a fencing display, or some other nondramatic exhibition. Weather conditions determined the season for the amphitheaters: plays were performed every day (including Sundays, sometimes, to clerical dismay) except during Lent – the forty days before Easter – or periods of plague, or sometimes during the summer months when law courts were not in session and the most affluent members of the audience were not in London.

To a modern theatergoer, an amphitheater stage like that of the Rose or Globe would appear an unfamiliar mixture of plainness and elaborate decoration. Much of the structure was carved or painted, sometimes to imitate marble; elsewhere, as under the canopy projecting over the stage, to represent the stars and the zodiac. Appropriate painted canvas pictures (of Jerusalem, for example, if the play was set in that city) were apparently hung on the wall behind the acting area, and tragedies were accompanied by black hangings, presumably something like crepe festoons or bunting. Although these theaters did not employ what we would call scenery, early modern spectators saw numerous large props, such as the "bar" at which a prisoner stood during a trial, the "mossy bank" where lovers reclined, an arbor for amorous conversation, a chariot, gallows, tables, trees, beds, thrones, writing desks, and so forth. Audiences might learn a scene's location from a sign (reading "Athens," for example) carried across the stage (as in Bertolt Brecht's twentieth-century productions). Equally captivating (and equally irritating to the theater's enemies) were the rich costumes and personal props the actors used: the most valuable items in the surviving theatrical inventories are the swords, gowns, robes, crowns, and other items worn or carried by the performers.

Magic appealed to Shakespeare's audiences as much as it does to us today, and the theater exploited many deceptive and spectacular devices. A winch in the loft above the stage, called "the heavens," could lower and raise actors playing gods, goddesses, and other supernatural figures to and from the main acting area, just as one or more trapdoors permitted entrances and exits to and from the area, called "hell," beneath the stage. Actors wore elementary makeup such as wigs, false beards, and face paint, and they employed pig's bladders filled with animal blood to make wounds seem more real. They had rudimentary but effective ways of pretending to behead or hang a person. Supernumeraries (stagehands or actors not needed in a particular scene) could make thunder sounds (by shaking a metal sheet or rolling an iron ball down a chute) and show lightning (by blowing inflammable resin through tubes into a flame). Elaborate fireworks enhanced the effects of dragons flying through the air or imitated such celestial phenomena as comets, shooting stars, and multiple suns. Horses' hoofbeats, bells (located perhaps in the tower above the stage), trumpets and drums, clocks, cannon shots and gunshots, and the like were common sound effects. And the music of viols, cornets, oboes, and recorders was a regular feature of theatrical performances.

For two relatively brief spans, from the late 1570s to 1590 and from 1599 to 1614, the amphitheaters competed with the so-called private, or indoor, theaters, which originated as, or later represented themselves as, educational institutions training boys as singers for church services and court performances. These indoor theaters had two features that were distinct from the amphitheaters': their personnel and their playing spaces. The amphitheaters' adult companies included both adult men, who played the male roles, and boys, who played the female roles; the private, or indoor, theater companies, on the other hand, were entirely composed of boys aged about 8 to 16, who were, or could pretend to be, candidates for singers in a church or a royal boys' choir. (Until 1660, professional theatrical companies included no women.) The playing space would appear much more familiar to modern audiences than the long-vanished amphitheaters; the later indoor theaters were, in fact, the ancestors of the typical modern theater. They were enclosed spaces, usually rectangular, with the stage filling one end of the rectangle and the audience arrayed in seats or benches across (and sometimes lining) the building's longer axis. These spaces staged plays less frequently than the public theaters (perhaps only once a week) and held far fewer spectators than the amphitheaters: about 200 to 600, as opposed to 2,500 or more. Fewer patrons mean a smaller gross income, unless each pays more. Not surprisingly, then, private theaters charged higher prices than the amphitheaters, probably sixpence, as opposed to a penny for the cheapest entry.

Protected from the weather, the indoor theaters presented plays later in the day than the amphitheaters, and used artificial illumination – candles in sconces or candelabra. But candles melt, and need replacing, snuffing, and trimming, and these practical requirements may have been part of the reason the indoor theaters introduced breaks in the performance, the intermission so dear to the heart of theatergoers and to the pocketbooks of theater concessionaires ever since. Whether motivated by the need to tend to the candles or by the entrepreneurs' wishing to sell oranges and liquor, or both, the indoor theaters eventually established the modern convention of the non-continuous performance. In the early modern "private" theater, musical performances apparently filled the intermissions, which in Stuart theater jargon seem to have been called "acts."

At the end of the first decade of the seventeenth century, the distinction between public amphitheaters and private indoor companies ceased. For various cultural, political, and economic reasons, individual companies gained control of both the public, open-air theaters and the indoor ones, and companies mixing adult men and boys took over the formerly "private" theaters. Despite the death of the boys' companies and of their highly innovative theaters (for which such luminous playwrights as Ben Jonson, George Chapman, and John Marston wrote), their playing spaces and conventions had an immense impact on subsequent plays: not merely for the intervals (which stressed the artistic and architectonic importance

of "acts"), but also because they introduced political and
social satire as a popular dramatic ingredient, even in
tragedy, and a wider range of actorly effects, encouraged
by their more intimate playing spaces.

Even the briefest sketch of the Shakespearean theatrical
world would be incomplete without some comment on the
social and cultural dimensions of theaters and playing in
the period. In an intensely hierarchical and status-
conscious society, professional actors and their ventures had
hardly any respectability; as we have indicated, to protect
themselves against laws designed to curb vagabondage and
the increase of masterless men, actors resorted to the near-
fiction that they were the servants of noble masters, and
wore their distinctive livery. Hence the company for which
Shakespeare wrote in the 1590s called itself the Lord
Chamberlain's Men and pretended that the public, money-
getting performances were in fact rehearsals for private performances before that high court official. From 1598, the
Privy Council had licensed theatrical companies, and after
1603, with the accession of King James I, the companies
gained explicit royal protection, just as the Queen's Men
had for a time under Queen Elizabeth. The Chamberlain's
Men became the King's Men, and the other companies
were patronized by the other members of the royal family.

These designations were legal fictions that half-
concealed an important economic and social development, the evolution away from the theater's organization
on the model of the guild, a self-regulating confraternity
of individual artisans, into a proto-capitalist organization.
Shakespeare's company became a joint-stock company,
where persons who supplied capital and, in some cases,
such as Shakespeare's, capital and talent, employed themselves and others in earning a return on that capital. This
development meant that actors and theater companies
were outside both the traditional guild structures, which
required some form of civic or royal charter, and the feu-
dal household organization of master-and-servant. This
anomalous, maverick social and economic condition

made theater companies practically unruly and potentially even dangerous; consequently, numerous official bodies – including the London metropolitan and ecclesiastical authorities as well as, occasionally, the royal court itself – tried, without much success, to control and even to disband them.

Public officials had good reason to want to close the theaters: they were attractive nuisances – they drew often riotous crowds, they were always noisy, and they could be politically offensive and socially insubordinate. Until the Civil War, however, anti-theatrical forces failed to shut down professional theater, for many reasons – limited surveillance and few police powers, tensions or outright hostilities among the agencies that sought to check or channel theatrical activity, and lack of clear policies for control. Another reason must have been the theaters' undeniable popularity. Curtailing any activity enjoyed by such a substantial percentage of the population was difficult, as various Roman emperors attempting to limit circuses had learned, and the Tudor-Stuart audience was not merely large, it was socially diverse and included women. The prevalence of public entertainment in this period has been underestimated. In fact, fairs, holidays, games, sporting events, the equivalent of modern parades, freak shows, and street exhibitions all abounded, but the theater was the most widely and frequently available entertainment to which people of every class had access. That fact helps account both for its quantity and for the fear and anger it aroused.

WILLIAM SHAKESPEARE OF STRATFORD-UPON-AVON, GENTLEMAN

Many people have said that we know very little about William Shakespeare's life – pinheads and postcards are often mentioned as appropriately tiny surfaces on which to record the available information. More imaginatively and perhaps more correctly, Ralph Waldo Emerson wrote, "Shakespeare is the only biographer of Shakespeare. . . . So far from Shakespeare's being the least known, he is the one person in all modern history fully known to us."

In fact, we know more about Shakespeare's life than we do about almost any other English writer's of his era. His last will and testament (dated March 25, 1616) survives, as do numerous legal contracts and court documents involving Shakespeare as principal or witness, and parish records in Stratford and London. Shakespeare appears quite often in official records of King James's royal court, and of course Shakespeare's name appears on numerous title pages and in the written and recorded words of his literary contemporaries Robert Greene, Henry Chettle, Francis Meres, John Davies of Hereford, Ben Jonson, and many others. Indeed, if we make due allowance for the bloating of modern, run-of-the-mill bureaucratic records, more information has survived over the past four hundred years about William Shakespeare of Stratford-upon-Avon, Warwickshire, than is likely to survive in the next four hundred years about any reader of these words.

What we do not have are entire categories of information – Shakespeare's private letters or diaries, drafts and revisions of poems and plays, critical prefaces or essays, commendatory verse for other writers' works, or instructions guiding his fellow actors in their performances, for instance – that we imagine would help us understand and appreciate his surviving writings. For all we know, many such data never existed as written records. Many literary and theatrical critics, not knowing what might once have existed, more or less cheerfully accept the situation; some even make a theoretical virtue of it by claiming that such data are irrelevant to understanding and interpreting the plays and poems.

So, what do we know about William Shakespeare, the man responsible for thirty-seven or perhaps more plays, more than 150 sonnets, two lengthy narrative poems, and some shorter poems?

While many families by the name of Shakespeare (or some variant spelling) can be identified in the English Midlands as far back as the twelfth century, it seems likely that the dramatist's grandfather, Richard, moved to Snitterfield, a town not far from Stratford-upon-Avon, sometime before 1529. In Snitterfield, Richard Shakespeare leased farmland from the very wealthy Robert Arden. By 1552, Richard's son John had moved to a large house on Henley Street in Stratford-upon-Avon, the house that stands today as "The Birthplace." In Stratford, John Shakespeare traded as a glover, dealt in wool, and lent money at interest; he also served in a variety of civic posts, including "High Bailiff," the municipality's equivalent of mayor. In 1557, he married Robert Arden's youngest daughter, Mary. Mary and John had four sons – William was the oldest – and four daughters, of whom only Joan outlived her most celebrated sibling. William was baptized (an event entered in the Stratford parish church records) on April 26, 1564, and it has become customary, without any good factual support, to suppose he was born on April 23, which happens to be the feast day of Saint George, patron saint of England, and is also the date on which he died, in 1616. Shakespeare married Anne Hathaway in 1582, when he was eighteen and she was twenty-six; their first child was born five months later. It has been generally assumed that the marriage was enforced and subsequently unhappy, but these are only assumptions; it has been estimated, for instance, that up to one third of Elizabethan brides were pregnant when they married. Anne and William Shakespeare had three children: Susanna, who married a prominent local physician, John Hall; and the twins Hamnet, who died young in 1596, and Judith, who married Thomas Quiney – apparently a rather shady individual. The name Hamnet was unusual but not unique: he and his twin sister were named for their godparents, Shakespeare's neighbors Hamnet and Judith Sadler. Shakespeare's father died in 1601 (the year of *Hamlet*), and Mary Arden Shakespeare died in 1608 (the year of *Coriolanus*). William Shakespeare's last surviving direct descendant was his granddaughter Elizabeth Hall, who died in 1670.

Between the birth of the twins in 1585 and a clear reference to Shakespeare as a practicing London dramatist in Robert Greene's sensationalizing, satiric pamphlet, *Greene's Groatsworth of Wit* (1592), there is no record of where William Shakespeare was or what he was doing. These seven so-called lost years have been imaginatively filled by scholars and other students of Shakespeare: some think he traveled to Italy, or fought in the Low Countries, or studied law or medicine, or worked as an apprentice actor/writer, and so on to even more fanciful possibilities. Whatever the biographical facts for those "lost" years, Greene's nasty remarks in 1592 testify to professional envy and to the fact that Shakespeare already had a successful career in London. Speaking to his fellow playwrights, Greene warns both generally and specifically:

> . . . trust them [actors] not: for there is an upstart crow, beautified with our feathers, that with his tiger's heart wrapped in a player's hide supposes he is as well able to bombast out a blank verse as the best of you; and being an absolute Johannes Factotum, is in his own conceit the only Shake-scene in a country.

The passage mimics a line from *3 Henry VI* (hence the play must have been performed before Greene wrote) and seems to say that "Shake-scene" is both actor and playwright, a jack-of-all-trades. That same year, Henry Chettle protested Greene's remarks in *Kind-Heart's Dream*, and each of the next two years saw the publication of poems – *Venus and Adonis* and *The Rape of Lucrece*, respectively – publicly ascribed to (and dedicated by) Shakespeare. Early in 1595 he was named as one of the senior members of a prominent acting company, the Lord Chamberlain's Men, when they received payment for court performances during the 1594 Christmas season.

Clearly, Shakespeare had achieved both success and reputation in London. In 1596, upon Shakespeare's application, the College of Arms granted his father the now-familiar coat of arms he had taken the first steps to obtain almost twenty years before, and in 1598, John's son – now permitted to call himself "gentleman" – took a 10 percent share in the new Globe playhouse. In 1597, he bought a substantial bourgeois house, called New Place, in Stratford – the garden remains, but Shakespeare's house, several times rebuilt, was torn down in 1759 – and over the next few years Shakespeare spent large sums buying land and making other investments in the town and its environs. Though he worked in London, his family remained in Stratford, and he seems always to have considered Stratford the home he would eventually return to. Something approaching a disinterested appreciation of Shakespeare's popular and professional status appears in Francis Meres's *Palladis Tamia* (1598), a not especially imaginative and perhaps therefore persuasive record of literary reputations. Reviewing contemporary English writers, Meres lists the titles of many of Shakespeare's plays, including one not now known, *Love's Labor's Won,* and praises his "mellifluous & hony-tongued" "sugred Sonnets," which were then circulating in manuscript (they were first collected in 1609). Meres describes Shakespeare as "one of the best" English playwrights of both comedy and tragedy. In *Remains . . . Concerning Britain* (1605), William Camden – a more authoritative source than the imitative Meres – calls Shakespeare one of the "most pregnant witts of these our times" and joins him with such writers as Chapman, Daniel, Jonson, Marston, and Spenser. During the first decades of the seventeenth century, publishers began to attribute numerous play quartos, including some non-Shakespearean ones, to Shakespeare, either by name or initials, and we may assume that they deemed Shakespeare's name and supposed authorship, true or false, commercially attractive.

For the next ten years or so, various records show

Shakespeare's dual career as playwright and man of the theater in London, and as an important local figure in Stratford. In 1608-9 his acting company – designated the "King's Men" soon after King James had succeeded Queen Elizabeth in 1603 – rented, refurbished, and opened a small interior playing space, the Blackfriars theater, in London, and Shakespeare was once again listed as a substantial sharer in the group of proprietors of the playhouse. By May 11, 1612, however, he describes himself as a Stratford resident in a London lawsuit – an indication that he had withdrawn from day-to-day professional activity and returned to the town where he had always had his main financial interests. When Shakespeare bought a substantial residential building in London, the Blackfriars Gatehouse, close to the theater of the same name, on March 10, 1613, he is recorded as William Shakespeare "of Stratford upon Avon in the county of Warwick, gentleman," and he named several London residents as the building's trustees. Still, he continued to participate in theatrical activity: when the new Earl of Rutland needed an allegorical design to bear as a shield, or *impresa*, at the celebration of King James's Accession Day, March 24, 1613, the earl's accountant recorded a payment of 44 shillings to Shakespeare for the device with its motto.

For the last few years of his life, Shakespeare evidently concentrated his activities in the town of his birth. Most of the final records concern business transactions in Stratford, ending with the notation of his death on April 23, 1616, and burial in Holy Trinity Church, Stratford-upon-Avon.

THE QUESTION OF AUTHORSHIP

The history of ascribing Shakespeare's plays (the poems do not come up so often) to someone else began, as it continues, peculiarly. The earliest published claim that someone else wrote Shakespeare's plays appeared in an 1856 article by Delia Bacon in the American journal *Putnam's Monthly* – although an Englishman, Thomas Wilmot, had shared his doubts in private (even secretive) conversations with friends near the end of the eighteenth century. Bacon's was a sad personal history that ended in madness and poverty, but the year after her article, she published, with great difficulty and the bemused assistance of Nathaniel Hawthorne (then United States Consul in Liverpool, England), her *Philosophy of the Plays of Shakspere Unfolded.* This huge, ornately written, confusing farrago is almost unreadable; sometimes its intents, to say nothing of its arguments, disappear entirely beneath near-raving, ecstatic writing. Tumbled in with much supposed "philosophy" appear the claims that Francis Bacon (from whom Delia Bacon eventually claimed descent), Walter Ralegh, and several other contemporaries of Shakespeare's had written the plays. The book had little impact except as a ridiculed curiosity.

Once proposed, however, the issue gained momentum among people whose conviction was the greater in proportion to their ignorance of sixteenth- and seventeenth-century English literature, history, and society. Another American amateur, Catherine P. Ashmead Windle, made the next influential contribution to the cause when she published *Report to the British Museum* (1882), wherein she promised to open "the Cipher of Francis Bacon," though what she mostly offers, in the words of S. Schoenbaum, is "demented allegorizing." An entire new cottage industry grew from Windle's suggestion that the texts contain hidden, cryptographically discoverable ciphers – "clues" – to their authorship; and today there are not only books devoted to the putative ciphers, but also pamphlets, journals, and newsletters.

Although Baconians have led the pack of those seeking a substitute Shakespeare, in *"Shakespeare" Identified* (1920), J. Thomas Looney became the first published

"Oxfordian" when he proposed Edward de Vere, seventeenth earl of Oxford, as the secret author of Shakespeare's plays. Also for Oxford and his "authorship" there are today dedicated societies, articles, journals, and books. Less popular candidates – Queen Elizabeth and Christopher Marlowe among them – have had adherents, but the movement seems to have divided into two main contending factions, Baconian and Oxfordian. (For further details on all the candidates for "Shakespeare," see S. Schoenbaum, *Shakespeare's Lives,* 2nd ed., 1991.)

The Baconians, the Oxfordians, and supporters of other candidates have one trait in common – they are snobs. Every pro-Bacon or pro-Oxford tract sooner or later claims that the historical William Shakespeare of Stratford-upon-Avon could not have written the plays because he could not have had the training, the university education, the experience, and indeed the imagination or background their author supposedly possessed. Only a learned genius like Bacon or an aristocrat like Oxford could have written such fine plays. (As it happens, lucky male children of the middle class had access to better education than most aristocrats in Elizabethan England – and Oxford was not particularly well educated.) Shakespeare received in the Stratford grammar school a formal education that would daunt many college graduates today; and popular rival playwrights such as the very learned Ben Jonson and George Chapman, both of whom also lacked university training, achieved great artistic success, without being taken as Bacon or Oxford.

Besides snobbery, one other quality characterizes the authorship controversy: lack of evidence. A great deal of testimony from Shakespeare's time shows that Shakespeare wrote Shakespeare's plays and that his contemporaries recognized them as distinctive and distinctly superior. (Some of that contemporary evidence is collected in E. K. Chambers, *William Shakespeare: A Study of Facts and Problems,* 2 vols., 1930.) Since that testimony comes from Shakespeare's enemies and theatrical competitors as well as from his co-workers and from the Elizabethan equivalent of literary journalists, it seems unlikely that, if any of these sources had known he was a fraud, they would have failed to record that fact.

Books About Shakespeare's Theater

Useful scholarly studies of theatrical life in Shakespeare's day include: G. E. Bentley, *The Jacobean and Caroline Stage*, 7 vols. (1941-68), and the same author's *The Professions of Dramatist and Player in Shakespeare's Time, 1590-1642* (1986); E. K. Chambers, *The Elizabethan Stage*, 4 vols. (1923); R. A. Foakes, *Illustrations of the English Stage, 1580-1642* (1985); Andrew Gurr, *The Shakespearean Stage*, 3rd ed. (1992), and the same author's *Play-going in Shakespeare's London,* 2nd ed. (1996); Edwin Nungezer, *A Dictionary of Actors* (1929); Carol Chillington Rutter, ed., *Documents of the Rose Playhouse* (1984).

Books About Shakespeare's Life

The following books provide scholarly, documented accounts of Shakespeare's life: G. E. Bentley, *Shakespeare: A Biographical Handbook* (1961); E. K. Chambers, *William Shakespeare: A Study of Facts and Problems,* 2 vols. (1930); S. Schoenbaum, *William Shakespeare: A Compact Documentary Life* (1977); and *Shakespeare's Lives,* 2nd ed. (1991), by the same author. Many scholarly editions of Shakespeare's complete works print brief compilations of essential dates and events. References to Shakespeare's works up to 1700 are collected in C. M. Ingleby et al., *The Shakespeare Allusion-Book,* rev. ed., 2 vols. (1932).

The Texts of Shakespeare

As far as we know, only one manuscript conceivably in Shakespeare's own hand may (and even this is much disputed) exist: a few pages of a play called *Sir Thomas More*, which apparently was never performed. What we do have, as later readers, performers, scholars, students, are printed texts. The earliest of these survive in two forms: quartos and folios. Quartos (from the Latin for "four") are small books, printed on sheets of paper that were then folded in fours, to make eight double-sided pages. When these were bound together, the result was a squarish, eminently portable volume that sold for the relatively small sum of sixpence (translating in modern terms to about $5.00). In folios, on the other hand, the sheets are folded only once, in half, producing large, impressive volumes taller than they are wide. This was the format for important works of philosophy, science, theology, and literature (the major precedent for a folio Shakespeare was Ben Jonson's *Works*, 1616). The decision to print the works of a popular playwright in folio is an indication of how far up on the social scale the theatrical profession had come during Shakespeare's lifetime. The Shakespeare folio was an expensive book, selling for between fifteen and eighteen shillings, depending on the binding (in modern terms, from about $150 to $180). Twenty Shakespeare plays of the thirty-seven that survive first appeared in quarto, seventeen of which appeared during Shakespeare's lifetime; the rest of the plays are found only in folio.

The First Folio was published in 1623, seven years after Shakespeare's death, and was authorized by his fellow actors, the co-owners of the King's Men. This publication was certainly a mark of the company's enormous respect for Shakespeare; but it was also a way of turning the old plays, most of which were no longer current in the play-house, into ready money (the folio includes only Shake-speare's plays, not his sonnets or other nondramatic verse). Whatever the motives behind the publication of the folio, the texts it preserves constitute the basis for almost all later editions of the playwright's works. The texts, however, differ from those of the earlier quartos, sometimes in minor respects but often significantly – most strikingly in the two texts of *King Lear,* but also in important ways in *Hamlet, Othello,* and *Troilus and Cressida.* (The variants are recorded in the textual notes to each play in the new Pelican series.) The differences in these texts represent, in a sense, the essence of theater: the texts of plays were initially not intended for publication. They were scripts, designed for the actors to perform – the principal life of the play at this period was in performance. And it follows that in Shakespeare's theater the playwright typically had no say either in how his play was performed or in the disposition of his text – he was an employee of the company. The authoritative figures in the theatrical enterprise were the shareholders in the company, who were for the most part the major actors. They decided what plays were to be done; they hired the playwright and often gave him an outline of the play they wanted him to write. Often, too, the play was a collaboration: the company would retain a group of writers, and parcel out the scenes among them. The resulting script was then the property of the company, and the actors would revise it as they saw fit during the course of putting it on stage. The resulting text belonged to the company. The playwright had no rights in it once he had been paid. (This system survives largely intact in the movie industry, and most of the playwrights of Shakespeare's time were as anonymous as most screenwriters are today.) The script could also, of course, continue to change as the tastes of audiences and the requirements of the actors changed. Many – perhaps most – plays were revised when they were reintroduced after any substantial absence from the repertory, or when they were performed by a company different from the one that originally commissioned the play.

Shakespeare was an exceptional figure in this world because he was not only a shareholder and actor in his company, but also its leading playwright – he was literally his own boss. He had, moreover, little interest in the publication of his plays, and even those that appeared during his lifetime with the authorization of the company show no signs of any editorial concern on the part of the author. Theater was, for Shakespeare, a fluid and supremely responsive medium – the very opposite of the great classic canonical text that has embodied his works since 1623.

The very fluidity of the original texts, however, has meant that Shakespeare has always had to be edited. Here is an example of how problematic the editorial project inevitably is, a passage from the most famous speech in *Romeo and Juliet*, Juliet's balcony soliloquy beginning "O Romeo, Romeo, wherefore art thou Romeo?" Since the eighteenth century, the standard modern text has read,

> What's Montague? It is nor hand, nor foot,
> Nor arm, nor face, nor any other part
> Belonging to a man. O be some other name!
> What's in a name? That which we call a rose
> By any other name would smell as sweet.
>
> (II.2.40-44)

Editors have three early texts of this play to work from, two quarto texts and the folio. Here is how the First Quarto (1597) reads:

> Whats *Mountague*? It is nor hand nor foote,
> Nor arme, nor face, nor any other part.
> Whats in a name? That which we call a Rose,
> By any other name would smell as sweet:

Here is the Second Quarto (1599):

> Whats *Mountague*? it is nor hand nor foote,
> Nor arme nor face, ô be some other name
> Belonging to a man.
> Whats in a name that which we call a rose,
> By any other word would smell as sweete,

And here is the First Folio (1623):

> What's *Mountague*? it is nor hand nor foote,
> Nor arme, nor face, O be some other name
> Belonging to a man.
> What? in a names that which we call a Rose,
> By any other word would smell as sweete,

There is in fact no early text that reads as our modern text does – and this is the most famous speech in the play. Instead, we have three quite different texts, all of which are clearly some version of the same speech, but none of which seems to us a final or satisfactory version. The transcendently beautiful passage in modern editions is an editorial invention: editors have succeeded in conflating and revising the three versions into something we recognize as great poetry. Is this what Shakespeare "really" wrote? Who can say? What we can say is that Shakespeare always had performance, not a book, in mind.

Books About the Shakespeare Texts

The standard study of the printing history of the First Folio is W. W. Greg, *The Shakespeare First Folio* (1955). J. K. Walton, *The Quarto Copy for the First Folio of Shakespeare* (1971), is a useful survey of the relation of the quartos to the folio. The second edition of Charlton Hinman's *Norton Facsimile* of the First Folio (1996), with a new introduction by Peter Blayney, is indispensable. Stanley Wells, Gary Taylor, John Jarrett, and William Montgomery, *William Shakespeare: A Textual Companion,* keyed to the Oxford text, gives a comprehensive survey of the editorial situation for all the plays and poems.

THE GENERAL EDITORS

Introduction

THE MERCHANT OF VENICE was being performed, it seems, in London during the late summer of 1598. As Shakespeare composed the play, he combined two much older narratives, the "flesh-bond" plot (sometimes called the "hate plot") and the "casket-test" plot (also called the "love plot"). Joining these plots proved both fertile and troublesome because the plots do not easily coexist. Shakespeare's response to the plots' ungainly relation is both elegant and ambiguous. The elegance ranges from imaginative structural symmetries to the comic and cruel dialogue between Gobbo and son to the fairly gentle satire on the superficial all-male bonhomie that flutters around the melancholic merchant of Venice, Antonio. The ambiguities and the problems for the audience arise from the way the joined plots collapse ethics into commerce, morality into finance.

The first plot involves the wooing and winning of a rich woman, "the Lady of Belmonte" (a widow in Shakespeare's apparent source, *Il Pecorone*), who subsequently disguises herself as a lawyer to save her new husband's patron, Ansaldo (Antonio in the play), from an unnamed Jewish moneylender who had financed the wooing effort in return for a loan secured by a pound of Ansaldo's flesh. Like Portia, the disguised lady demands her husband's ring as compensation for her legal efforts and later demands, undisguised, that he explain its disappearance. Ser Giovanni, a fourteenth-century Florentine writer, brought together even older narrative elements to make the short story that Shakespeare adopted and further changed. Shakespeare's principal change – if some now-unknown author had not made it first – was to substitute the casket test, a very old folkloric love trial, for Ser Giovanni's device, which involved winning the lady only by first having sexual intercourse with her – a feat she regularly evaded by drugging her suitors' wine and then seizing their property when they failed the test. Giannetto, the suitor in Ser Giovanni's story, fails twice before learning the secret of the drugged wine; his third and successful voyage to Belmonte exposes Ansaldo, who is Giannetto's godfather, to the moneylender's flesh demand.

Replacing the sex-and-drugs portion of Ser Giovanni's narrative with the casket test meant providing a new past for many of the central characters. It meant, for example: changing the circumstances of the lady, who now is both never-married and chaste; changing the motivations of Ansaldo-Antonio; crucially, it meant inventing an *origin* for the casket test. It meant, that is, inventing Portia's dead father – "In Belmont is a lady richly *left*" (I.1.161, my italics) – and consequently raising large issues of patriarchal control and filial duty:

> I may neither choose who I would nor refuse who
> I dislike, so is the will of a living daughter curbed
> by the will of a dead father.
>
> (I.2.22-24)

Portia goes on to ask, "Is it not hard, Nerissa, that I cannot choose one, nor refuse none?" (24-25), and indeed it does seem very odd, especially after Nerissa's unconvincing answer, that Portia's life mate should be determined by "lottery" (27-28). The chance-determined test is, as Portia later says, "the lott'ry of my destiny / [It] Bars me the right of voluntary choosing" (II.1.15-16). The changes Shakespeare made in his source text threaten our sense of Portia's independence; the changes obscure the relation between Bassanio and Antonio, which is no longer based in familial ties but rests on a murkily sketched friendship that has seemed to many critics and producers to be at least partly homosexual. Finally, these changes risk making Bassanio even more avaricious than his source model Giannetto without satisfactorily adding loyal friendship to his qualities.

Shakespeare's comic dramaturgy delights in similarities-with-differences, parallels that are illuminatingly askew. The disturbing partial parallels to Portia's situation include Shylock's daughter Jessica; Portia's waiting gentlewoman Nerissa; and (oddest of all) Shylock's servant Lancelot Gobbo. Jessica, whose "house is hell" and who is "ashamed to be" her "father's child" (II.3.2,17), finally elopes with her future husband – "I have a father, you a daughter, lost" (II.5.56). Or, the play allows us to feel that she is abducted both physically and spiritually; she says she "Did . . . steal from the wealthy Jew" (a painful term for her father), and Lorenzo describes his act as "Stealing her soul" (V.1.15,19). Gratiano gains Nerissa more abruptly than Bassanio wins Portia, but he does so as a result of the very same lottery:

> You saw the mistress, I beheld the maid.
> You loved, I loved . . .
> *　*　*　*　*　*　*　*
> Your fortune stood upon the caskets there,
> And so did mine too as the matter falls.
> *　*　*　*　*　*　*　*
> With oaths of love, at last – if promise last –
> I got a promise of this fair one here
> To have her love, provided that your fortune
> Achieved her mistress.
> (III.2.198-99, 201-2, 205-8)

Lancelot Gobbo, with whom Jessica exchanges more lines than with any other character, is an employee like Nerissa, and, like Jessica, he seeks to escape Shylock's house by any means, fair or foul:

> Certainly my conscience will serve me to run from this Jew my master. . . . To be ruled by my con-

> science, I should stay with the Jew my master
> who, God bless the mark, is a kind of devil; and to
> run away from the Jew, I should be ruled by the
> fiend who, saving your reverence, is the devil him-
> self.
>
> (II.2.1-2, 20-24)

Lancelot resolves his comic quandary – he sees the devil
wherever he looks, even in his own conscience – by
getting his "true-begotten father" (32-33) to help him
change masters, as indeed Elizabethan custom would en-
dorse. The exchange of one master for another through a
father's mediation literalizes, however, some ambiguous
parallels among Lancelot, Portia, Jessica, and Nerissa. Fathers, husbands, and fiancés are versions of the master;
daughters and wives, of the servant.

Shakespeare's inventions to make the casket test work
may be seen elsewhere in his romantic comedies (indeed,
many came from classical Roman comedy): daughters
often have trouble with their fathers' marital choices;
friends, relatives, or waiting women often fall in love apparently because their friends, relatives, or mistresses have
fallen in love; servants' experiences often run alongside
the wealthier or more elite characters' experiences. And
these parallels also operate in *The Merchant of Venice* to
make the wooing plots intercommunicate with the flesh-
bond plot in ways that generally make the love issues less
frivolous than they might first appear and Shylock less
monomaniacal than the Jewish moneylender in Shakespeare's source.

Changing the way Bassanio gains Portia also meant
changing the original narrative's relation between Bassanio and Antonio; both those sets of changes also en-
tailed, at least for Shakespeare, changes in the flesh-bond
plot, especially in the motivation of the moneylender,
whose original in Ser Giovanni's story was as stereotypi-
cally and anti-Semitically Jewish as the Bassanio figure
was a playboy-adventurer and the Portia figure was a

greedy sexual stereotype. Shakespeare's original audiences had little or no direct knowledge of Jews and Jewish practices or, for that matter, international financiers of any national or ethnic origin. Shakespeare himself probably had not much more. What Shakespeare and his audiences certainly shared was stereotypical, even mythic, "knowledge," and in particular they would, or could, have known three quite striking Jewish dramatic characters linked with money: Gerontus in Robert Wilson's *The Three Ladies of London* (performed about 1581, published 1584); Barabas in Christopher Marlowe's immensely popular and vigorous *The Jew of Malta* (performed about 1589, published 1633); Pisaro in William Haughton's *Englishmen for My Money* (composed 1598, published 1616).*

Gerontus and Pisaro illustrate unexpected features of Shylock's theatrical heritage. Gerontus is an unequivocally good character who appears in a few brief scenes set in the Turkish empire; there, he demands the long-overdue repayment of his loan to the Italian Mercadorus (i.e., a version of "Merchant" in mangled Spanish or Italian) and is first stalled, then refused. When the matter goes to trial and Gerontus is upheld, Mercadorus decides to renounce Christianity for Islam, an act that would legally clear all debts. Rather than force a religious conversion, Gerontus forgives the debt, and the Turkish judge concludes, "as appears by this / Jews seek to excel in Christianity, and Christians in Jewishness." This highly ambivalent remark combines anti-Judaism with English anti-Catholicism and xenophobia – if we assume Mercadorus is meant to be Roman Catholic as well as Italian. The dialogue is otherwise remarkably free of anti-Jewish slurs, though Venice is described as "a city / Where Usury by Lucre [Money] may live in great glory" and "aliens" (foreigners to England) are heavily criticized.

---

* *The Jew of Malta* is quoted from N. W. Bawcutt's Revels Plays edition (Manchester: Manchester University Press, 1978); the other plays mentioned here are quoted from the original quartos, slightly modernized.

If good Gerontus is a means to attack bad, indeed rene-gade, Christians, as Shylock also seems to be and Mar-lowe's Barabas certainly is, then Haughton's Pisaro, a Portuguese moneylender and merchant obliquely charac-terized as a Jew, illustrates another side of the theatrical heritage, for he is father to not one, but three, marriage-able daughters. Shakespeare's contemporaries, playwrights and audiences alike, thought that tricking rich old men out of their daughters was even funnier than tricking them out of their money; if a young man – or in the case of Haughton's play, *three* young men – could connive his way out of debt to the old man and into marriage with his daughter, so much the better and funnier. And if, as in Haughton's play, the young men simultaneously beat the old man's favored (and foreign!) suitors, so very much the better. Clearly, the emphasis in *Englishmen for My Money* falls on intergenerational trickery and sexual desire that are as old, theatrically, as classical Greek and Roman com-edy. The play's anti-money, anti-moneylending, anti-alien (as Shylock is – IV.1.347), and anti-Jewish elements do show how Lorenzo's elopement-abduction and how Salarino and Solanio's obscene crowing (II.8) over Shy-lock's loss of daughter and ducats could grow from tradi-tional comic roots.

More overtly and coarsely than Shylock, Barabas serves as a means to attack Christian hypocrisy, sanctimony, and lack of charity. Like Shylock and his daughter, Jessica, Marlowe's Barabas has a beloved daughter, Abigail, who loves a gentile and who twice converts – once falsely, then truly – to Christianity. The fathers and their daughters in the two plays are often quite similar, and Shakespeare is cer-tainly nodding to Marlowe's play when Shylock exclaims, "These be the Christian husbands! I have a daughter; / Would any of the stock of Barabbas / Had been her hus-band, rather than a Christian!" (IV.1.293-95; Shake-speare uses another spelling of the biblical name). Yet it is the differences between the plays that matter more than the similarities, at least to a modern audience. Marlowe's

Barabas begins as a briefly sympathetic victim but evolves into an increasingly hysterical caricature – a zany, wickedly funny, homicidal (in truth, genocidal), immensely intelligent, and realistically implausible creation who runs through in five acts practically all the choices actors have made over the centuries for Shylock: comic monster, buffoon, tragic victim, flawed and overwronged ordinary human, sadistic genius. Barabas represents a series of extremes the stereotypical Jew in drama, legend, and folklore could and did become, although he is the only instance of virtually all those possibilities in a single character.

A few examples will illustrate how Barabas and *The Jew of Malta* might have served as a quarry for the very different character and play Shakespeare created. Both Barabas and Shylock are deeply and proudly conscious of their descent from "father Abram" and their membership in "our sacred nation" (I.3.158, 45) or, as Barabas says, "unto us the promise doth belong" (II.3.48). Barabas refers to the covenant between Abraham and God (Genesis 17:1-22), but the writings of Paul (e.g., Galatians 3:13-16) and patristic theologians had worked strenuously to transfer the promise of spiritual happiness, as opposed to worldly success, from the Jews to those who believed in Jesus Christ.*

Religious pride serves as a terrible spur for both Barabas and Shylock. At the start of what proves a killing spree, Barabas masterminds the death of Abigail's gentile lover. When she learns of her father's duplicity, she flees to a Christian convent, where he manages to kill her and all the nuns beside. Shylock, too, expresses horror at his daughter's flight and conversion – "She is damned for it. . . . My own flesh and blood to rebel!" (III.1.29, 31) – but the closest Shylock comes to Barabas's act is his terrible curse:

---

* See "The Theology of *The Jew of Malta*" (1964) in G. K. Hunter, *Dramatic Identities and Cultural Tradition* (New York: Barnes and Noble, 1978), pp. 64–70.

> A diamond gone cost me two thousand ducats in
> Frankfurt! The curse never fell upon our nation
> till now; I never felt it till now. Two thousand
> ducats in that, and other precious, precious jewels.
> I would my daughter were dead at my foot, and
> the jewels in her ear! Would she were hearsed at
> my foot, and the ducats in her coffin.
>
> (III.1.77-83)

While this curse is very far from Barabas's mass murder,
Shylock shares with him the vaunting egomania that
equates an act of filial impiety with the "curse . . . upon
our nation," presumably the prophecy of Jerusalem's destruction in Matthew 23:38. That is, one daughter's dis-
obedience her father understands as an entire nation's
destruction. And the mourned loss is not the daughter,
but the ducats and the diamond. Shylock finely measures
his loss. His delicate precision, if that is not too horrifying
a phrase, defines the distance between Barabas's grandiose
violence, so terrible as to be comically unbelievable and
unacceptable as fact, and Shakespeare's thought-through,
human response to Jessica's betrayal of religion and father.
Abigail had earlier pleased her father by helping him re-
cover part of his fortune, and his alliterative response –
"O girl, O gold, O beauty, O my bliss" (II.1.53) –
prompted Shylock's despairing " 'My daughter! O my
ducats! O my daughter! . . . My ducats and my daughter!' "
(II.8.15-17). By inserting "and" into the alliterative series,
Shakespeare moves from Marlowe's equation of daughter
and money to a more complicated sense of the moneylender's loss: daughter *and* money rather than daughter
as money.

   Just how persons are to be valued and how they receive
or forfeit value are among the play's most troubling and
unsettled questions. Plainly, the gruesome horror of the
Antonio-Shylock agreement puts a specific price on
human flesh: one pound costs three thousand ducats. The
parallel in *The Jew of Malta* is Barabas's purchase of a

slave, and Shylock stresses the connection between his flesh collateral and (Christian) human slavery:

> You have among you [Venetians] many a pur-
>   chased slave,
> Which like your asses and your dogs and mules
> You use in abject and in slavish parts,
> Because you bought them. Shall I say to you,
> "Let them be free! Marry them to your heirs!
> Why sweat they under burdens? Let their beds
> Be made as soft as yours, and let their palates
> Be seasoned with such viands"? You will answer,
> "The slaves are ours." So do I answer you.
> The pound of flesh which I demand of him
> Is dearly bought, 'tis mine, and I will have it.
>   (IV.1.90–100)

From such bluntly painful unions of flesh and cost, or flesh and price, it is a small step into half-metaphorical links between money and what is "fair":

> In Belmont is a lady richly left;
> And she is fair, and fairer than that word,
> Of wondrous virtues. Sometimes from her eyes
> I did receive fair speechless messages.
> Her name is Portia, nothing undervalued
> To Cato's daughter, Brutus' Portia;
> Nor is the wide world ignorant of her worth,
> For the four winds blow in from every coast
> Renownèd suitors, and her sunny locks
> Hang on her temples like a golden fleece,
> Which makes her seat of Belmont Colchos' strand,
> And many Jasons come in quest of her.
> O my Antonio, had I but the means
> To hold a rival place with one of them,
> I have a mind presages me such thrift
> That I should questionless be fortunate!
>   (I.1.161–76)

No doubt, Bassanio here lists Portia's qualities – "richly left," "fair" (i.e., beautiful), "Of wondrous virtues" – in an increasing series, which values her "virtues" last and highest. The audience hears first, however, Portia's wealth in money, not virtues, and the rest of the speech wobbles among words that could represent either (or both) crass greed and high, virtuous praise: "her worth," "sunny locks . . . like a golden fleece," "means," "thrift," "fortunate."

Thus, the play links money and "fair" (Portia). It also links money and "good" (Antonio):

> SHYLOCK   Three thousand ducats for three months, and Antonio bound.
> BASSANIO   Your answer to that.
> SHYLOCK   Antonio is a good man.
> BASSANIO   Have you heard any imputation to the contrary?
> SHYLOCK   Ho no, no, no, no! My meaning in saying he is a good man is to have you understand me that he is sufficient. Yet his means are in supposition.
>
> (I.3.9-17)

Quite deliberately, or so it seems, Shylock introduces "good" to create an ambiguity. Is Antonio "good," an honorable and virtuous man, or is he "sufficient" – "good" for the value of the loan? Once the audience's thoughts are turned this way, at least two other troubling ideas may occur. Must there be a conflict between virtue and financial sufficiency (i.e., may Antonio be "good" in only one of the two meanings)? And, more literally, will Antonio's body prove "sufficient" to pay the "forfeit" Shylock will soon propose, "an equal pound / Of your fair flesh" (147-48)?

For all the play's notorious emphasis on religious difference, economic difference is more powerful:

> How like a fawning publican he [Antonio] looks.
> I hate him for he is a Christian;

But more, for that in low simplicity
He lends out money gratis and brings down
The rate of usance here with us in Venice.
If I catch him once upon the hip,
I will feed fat the ancient grudge I bear him.
He hates our sacred nation, and he rails,
Even there where merchants most do congregate,
On me, my bargains, and my well-won thrift,
Which he calls interest. Cursèd be my tribe
If I forgive him.

(38-49)

Shylock regards hating Antonio as a given – "for he is a Christian." A greater motive for hatred is financial and competitive – "He lends out money gratis and brings down / The rate of usance here with us [i.e., Jews who lend at interest] in Venice." And, at least according to Shylock, Antonio feels the same way, converting economic antagonism into the language of religious intolerance:

Signor Antonio, many a time and oft
In the Rialto you have rated me
About my moneys and my usances.
    *   *   *   *   *   *   *
You call me misbeliever, cutthroat dog,
And spit upon my Jewish gaberdine,
And all for use of that which is mine own.
(103-5, 108-10)

Shylock then sarcastically repeats Antonio's insults, and Antonio agrees, "I am as like to call thee so again, / To spit on thee again, to spurn thee too" (127-28). Shylock now feigns (?) surprise at Antonio's anger ("how you storm") and claims he would "Forget the shames that you have stained me with" (136) – plainly untrue for either character – and that what he offers Antonio is kindly: "This is kind I offer" (139). And Bassanio, apparently without irony or wit, agrees: "This were kindness." Ambi-

guities in Elizabethan "kind," which could have the modern meaning of "benevolent, helpful" and also the
stronger meanings "natural" and "nature," make these
highly fraught exchanges. Bassanio may take the flesh-
bond offer at its surface meaning, a benevolent gesture, "a
merry sport" as Shylock calls it (143); another, more gruesome but more likely set of meanings underlies "This is
kind I offer": economic competition is "natural" to hu-
mankind, as is religious hatred, as is the desire for an
enemy's death. When Shylock departs for dinner at Bassanio's house, it is hard not to hear cannibalistic under-
tones:

> I am not bid for love, they flatter me;
> But yet I'll go in hate to feed upon
> The prodigal Christian.
>
> (II.5.13-15)

Shylock has dismissed the possibility earlier – "A pound
of man's flesh . . . Is not so estimable . . . As flesh of muttons, beefs, or goats" (I.3.163-65) – but he returns to it
when he congratulates himself on passing the "huge
feeder" Lancelot, whom he endearingly likes, to Bassanio
because "I would have him help to waste / His borrowed
purse" (II.5.49-50). Lancelot no longer feeds on Shylock
but on the money Antonio borrowed from Shylock and
lent to Bassanio; hence, Lancelot "feeds on" (eats at the
expense of) Bassanio, and Shylock will consume Bassanio's feast and his benefactor's flesh. Just as financial and
moral terminologies intermingle for Portia, her dead father, and Bassanio in the love plot, so do financial and
natural vocabularies in the hate plot.

The play, then, uses the facts and language of finance
and commerce to make the fact and language of morality,
values, and nature unstable and even tenuous. Shylock
and Antonio agree that commercial antipathy exceeds religious difference and hatred, and Bassanio's love cannot
escape a hint, at least, that it proceeds from avarice, or

self-interest. One of the play's most famous speeches, beginning "Hath not a Jew eyes?" is often taken out of context as Shakespeare's declaration of a common humanity that joins us all, Jew and gentile, slave and free, male and female (see Galatians 3:8). Yet, in context, the common trait is simply the desire for revenge:

> And if you wrong us, shall we not revenge? If we
> are like you in the rest, we will resemble you in
> that. If a Jew wrong a Christian, what is his humility? Revenge. If a Christian wrong a Jew, what
> should his sufferance be by Christian example?
> Why revenge! The villainy you teach me I will execute, and it shall go hard but I will better the instruction.
>
> (III.1.61-67)

In context, the speech traces a reciprocity of wrong, an escalation of revenge. To be human is not to recognize shared goods but to revenge exchanged wrongs, as Shylock's almost immediate response to his daughter's theft and elopement proves: "I would my daughter were dead at my foot, and the jewels in her ear!" (81-82). The ways religion, commerce, and humanity mingle in the Antonio-Shylock conflict also appear, as we have seen, in Salarino and Solanio's mocking account of Shylock's "passion so confused" when he learns of Jessica's elopement: "'O my ducats! O my daughter! . . . O my Christian ducats! . . . My ducats and my daughter!'" (II.8.15-17). Solanio's ominous later remark *connects* Lorenzo-Jessica with Shylock's loan: "Let good Antonio look he keep his day, / Or he shall pay for this" (25-26). That is, anger and antipathy will convert Shylock's loss of his daughter into rage against Antonio, as if Shylock had helped to rob himself and could compensate for losing Jessica by punishing "good Antonio" if he fails to "keep his day." Solanio's suspicion may not be logical, but the emotional analysis seems compelling and parallels the emotional

logic that makes religious and commercial hostility inter-
changeable and mutually reinforcing.

Antonio does not keep his day, and in a brief scene we
see him marched to jail at Shylock's insistence – "I'll have
my bond. I will not hear thee speak" (III.3.12) – and hear
Antonio acknowledge the link between not (this time)
commerce and religion but commerce and law:

> The duke cannot deny the course of law;
> For the commodity that strangers have
> With us in Venice, if it be denied,
> Will much impeach the justice of the state,
> Since that the trade and profit of the city
> Consisteth of all nations.
>
> (26–31)

Venice is a mercantile state; commercial honor, as well as
continued prosperity, requires evenhanded legal treat-
ment of citizen and alien alike. Antonio's grim conclusion, "These griefs and losses have so bated me / That I
shall hardly spare a pound of flesh / Tomorrow to my
bloody creditor" (32–34), follows the joyful scene (III.2)
in which Bassanio triumphantly passes the casket test and
wins Portia according to her dead father's lottery. Here,
then, at the play's center, the fortunes of the love plot and
hate plot balance – Bassanio victorious, Shylock seemingly so, Antonio hopeless.

Antonio's "tomorrow" arrives in the play's celebrated
"trial scene" (IV.1), more than 450 lines long and divided
into five unequal phases. The first phase establishes Shylock's intransigence and his admission that desiring Antonio's flesh cannot be rationalized:

> So can I give no reason, nor I will not,
> More than a lodged hate and a certain loathing
> I bear Antonio, that I follow thus
> A losing [i.e., unprofitable] suit against him.
>
> (59–62)

Bassanio offers money – "For thy three thousand ducats here is six" (84) – and the duke again pleads for mercy. All to no avail. Shakespeare follows his source's lead in the scene's second phase: Portia, disguised as Balthasar, "A young and learned doctor" of laws (144), is introduced by Nerissa "dressed as a lawyer's clerk," who represents "Bellario, a learned doctor" (105), from whom the Duke of Venice has requested help in deciding Shylock's case against Antonio. As the duke studies Bellario's letter introducing "Balthasar," Gratiano reviles Shylock: "harsh Jew, ... damned, inexecrable dog, ... thy desires / Are wolvish, bloody, starved, and ravenous" (123, 128, 137-38). So far the scene recapitulates what has gone before: Shylock's admittedly irrational insistence on a legal bond, pleas for mercy rather than strict justice, vilifications.

Portia's entrance, however, raises a significant performance question: how do we understand her behavior toward Shylock? The final 100 lines of Act III, scene 2 (the scene in which Bassanio chooses the lead casket and wins Portia in marriage) elaborately explain Antonio's peril, Shylock's obsession – "So keen and greedy to confound a man" (276) – and Bassanio's debt to, and love for, Antonio – "The dearest friend to me, the kindest man" (292). There, too, Portia first suggests the multiple repayment of the bond: "Pay him [Shylock] six thousand, and deface the bond. / Double six thousand and then treble that" (299-300). Portia, or "Balthasar," is as well informed about the circumstances as the audience is before she arrives at court: "I am informèd throughly of the cause" (IV.1.171). How then should a director present her next line, "Which is the merchant here and which the Jew?" Possible stagings include plain ignorance, disingenuousness, a kind of collusive smirking, or even aggressive prejudice. By this point, most (but not all) productions will have clearly distinguished Antonio from Shylock by costume, and their voices and behavior will certainly have distinguished the two actors from each other for the audience. Portia's question thus also raises an important performance decision for how these actors are to *react*.

These complexities make Portia's famous "The quality of mercy is not strained" (182-200), another speech often taken out of context, much less obviously the disinterested plea it might first appear. Rather, the speech may sound, or come to sound, like the opening salvo of a barrage that steadily forces Shylock to a louder and louder insistence on the bond and a growing certainty that Portia unequivocally supports his demand:

> My deeds upon my head! I crave the law,
> The penalty and forfeit of my bond.
> * * * * * * *
> A Daniel come to judgment! Yea, a Daniel!
> O wise young judge, how I do honor thee!
> * * * * * * *
> An oath, an oath! I have an oath in heaven!
> * * * * * * *
>   By my soul I swear
> There is no power in the tongue of man
> To alter me. I stay here on my bond.
>   (204-5, 221-22, 226, 238-40)

Once again, Bassanio – using Portia's money – offers "thrice the sum . . . ten times o'er" (208-9) and begs the court "To do a great right, do a little wrong." Once again, he is refused. After Portia establishes the mean details that Shylock has the "balance here to weigh / The flesh" but no surgeon "To stop his [Antonio's] wounds," the outcome appears determined, and Antonio delivers his farewell speech (262-79). Bassanio replies that he has a wife "as dear to me as life itself; / But life itself, my wife, and all the world / Are not with me esteemed above thy life" (281-83), and Portia momentarily reminds us that the play is, after all, also a comedy of disguise – "Your wife would give you little thanks . . . / If she were by."

All is ready for the "sentence" when Portia initiates the

third phase of the scene: "Tarry a little, there is something else. / This bond doth give thee here no jot of blood" (303-4). Shylock must have his pound of flesh,

> But in the cutting it if thou dost shed
> One drop of Christian blood, thy lands and goods
> Are by the laws of Venice confiscate
> Unto the state of Venice.
>
> (307-10)

While Gratiano jeeringly echoes Shylock's cries, "O upright judge! ... O learnèd judge!" (311), Shylock himself attempts to "take this offer then. Pay the bond thrice / And let the Christian go" (316-17). Portia refuses, and in a series of further denials duplicates Shylock's earlier insistence on the bond: "Thou shalt have nothing but the forfeiture, / To be so taken at thy peril, Jew" (341-42). The moment, for all the ugly sting of "Jew," is technically a comic climax: the threat to Antonio has been turned away harmlessly, neither blood nor ducat lost.

With Shylock stymied, comic momentum, the rising rhythm of jab and counterjab, requires his punishment, and it begins, as the scene's third phase had, with Portia's "Tarry" (344). She now proclaims he is guilty of intended murder – "by direct or indirect attempts" – and that one half of Shylock's goods is forfeited to his intended victim, Antonio, the other half to the state, and his life is to be at the duke's mercy. Shylock is forced into a humiliating compromise and required to accept Antonio's "mercy" (376). Shylock is forgiven his state fine on three conditions: the other half of his goods is to be given to Antonio in trust for Jessica and Lorenzo; "He presently become a Christian"; and his entire estate is to be bequeathed to Jessica and Lorenzo. That is, all of Shylock's property will sooner or later be Jessica and Lorenzo's. This financial arrangement merely defers the catastrophe Shylock foresaw when it seemed he was about to lose all instantly:

> Nay, take my life and all! Pardon not that!
> You take my house when you do take the prop
> That doth sustain my house; you take my life
> When you do take the means whereby I live.
> (372-75)

When Antonio announces his "mercy," these words ac-
crue meaning: "house," "prop," and "means" are not only
material, but religious and familial. The man who saw his
daughter's elopement as equivalent to the "curse . . . upon
our nation" (III.1.79) now sees his "house" – daughter
and ducats – descend to a gentile. Shylock's forced conversion also removes the "prop" that sustains "our sacred
nation" (I.3.45). Accepting these conditions, Shylock is
dismissed and exits the play for ever.

The famous "trial scene" is of course not a trial, and it
is possible to see it as something far nastier, a setup that
turns on a technicality (flesh, no blood) and then spite-
fully turns back on Shylock a legal rigidity he had been
duped into demanding. And all concludes with requiring
him to abandon his faith on pain of death. However re-
pugnant these vengeful acts appear to a modern audience,
history and dramatic genre should make us pause before
condemning Shakespeare, his play, and his characters. For
instance, the blood/flesh distinction that defeats Shylock's
agreement with Antonio has ample biblical precedent:
Genesis 9:4, Leviticus 7:26, Deuteronomy 12:23, Acts
15:29, among others. These Scriptural distinctions and
prohibitions gave rise to many important Judeo-Christian
practices. Considered as comic action, Act IV, scene 1 has
a long history in Western and Elizabethan drama. It ex-
emplifies what folklorists might call "The Biter Bit" –
Shylock, seemingly in command of his enemies, himself
becomes a victim through the very means he employed to
gain that victory, now empty and reversed upon him. Ben
Jonson's *Volpone, or The Fox* is a celebrated example
among plays by Shakespeare's contemporaries. Act IV,
scene 1 also calls upon an ancient comic convention –

what we call "the heavy father," a member of the older generation who wishes to control his offspring's choice of sexual partner. Traditionally, as in Haughton's *Englishmen for My Money* or in Shakespeare's *A Midsummer Night's Dream* and *The Tempest,* defeating the father liberates the child and frees the future to be different from the past. Finally, to understand how an Elizabethan audience might have understood Shylock's forced conversion, we must remember that such conversions were regarded as beneficent. Only converted could a Jew hope for (Christian) salvation, and Christian belief held that the "conversion of the Jews" (Andrew Marvell's phrase) would precede the end of time and the world's final turn to eternal joy (see Romans 11:11-12, 15-16, 25-26).

Historical and generic qualifications cannot and must not turn us aside from the play's most pressing issue for a modern audience: the consequences of the heavy father's, the Biter's, status as a Jew. Recent centuries have seen genocidal acts on every continent of the globe, and to distinguish one horror from another is to enter upon a morally revolting calculus. Most vivid of these events for a Western audience, however, is Nazi Germany's near-extermination of European Jews, and that horror alone makes it difficult – or impossible – to consider the Christian-Venetian vilification of Shylock dispassionately. Yes, Shakespeare's Shylock has a place in a dramatic, legendary, folkloric tradition of Jewish characters, some good, some bad, some just ordinarily a mixture of traits. And, yes, Shylock is a Jew and a father, a reviled individual and an economic man dedicated to profit and commercial triumph, a member of an ancient nation and an alien wherever he lives. And, yes, the play is of its time and place, for good and ill and both good *and* ill. Do these considerations free the historical playwright William Shakespeare from a (modern) charge of anti-Semitism? Who can say? I don't know. Those considerations have certainly not saved the play from being performed as anti-Jewish nor have they prevented its performance as a grand exposition of defiance and toleration, acceptance and celebration of difference.

Questions of anti-Semitism are among the freight that the flesh-bond plot brings and are thus chief among the ambiguities I mentioned at the beginning of this introduction. The play's compensatory elegance is part of the final phase of Act IV, scene 1, the joking over Bassanio's and Gratiano's rings, now given to Portia and Nerissa, which Shakespeare adopted from *Il Pecorone*. The rings represent marital fidelity, and their exchange reifies the eternal comic conflict between homosocial and heterosexual bonds. Is Antonio more important to Bassanio than Portia? Is Bassanio more important to Gratiano than Nerissa? This elegance extends to include the central physical facts of marriage in Act V, when the rings plainly symbolize the women's sexual organs:

> If you had known the virtue of the ring,
> Or half her worthiness that gave the ring,
> Or your own honor to contain the ring,
> You would not then have parted with the ring.
> What man is there so much unreasonable,
> If you had pleased to have defended it
> With any terms of zeal, wanted the modesty
> To urge the thing held as a ceremony?
> Nerissa teaches me what to believe:
> I'll die for't but some woman had the ring!
>   (V.1.199–208)

Bawdiness and comedy have long been intimate: the making of children and the perpetuation of society are among comedy's oldest concerns.

These final gritty jokes provide a pragmatic ground for the Fifth Act's high romance, the customary Shakespearean comic conclusion of reunion, reconciliation, and renewal. Moonlit and musical – "How sweet the moonlight sleeps upon this bank! / Here will we sit and let the sounds of music / Creep in our ears" (V.1.54–56) – Portia's estate in Belmont serves, we are asked to believe, as a refuge for the characters Venice and commerce have damaged, and as a nursery for society's improved future. As the act opens, Jessica and Lorenzo await Portia's return from her transvestite adventure, and as they wait they recall stories (from Ovid and Chaucer) of doomed lovers; they joke that they are not such lovers, that they will be happy and true, but the legendary disasters are only the first of many shadows cast across the play's conventionally happy ending. Still unaware of Portia and Nerissa's deception, Bassanio, Antonio, and the other men arrive from Venice, and the comedy of their ignorance and undeceiving ensues. Magically and offhandedly, Portia produces two letters; one explains the Balthasar deception, the other restores Antonio's fortune:

> Unseal this letter soon;
> There you shall find three of your argosies
> Are richly come to harbor suddenly.
> You shall not know by what strange accident
> I chancèd on this letter.
> (275–79)

Strange accidents are the lifeblood of Shakespearean romantic comedy, and it is hard to doubt that the playwright smilingly provided this letter, a graceful coup de théâtre, a scroll produced from offstage by an unseen hand. Nerissa adds a wonder we already know of:

> There do I give to you [Lorenzo] and Jessica
> From the rich Jew, a special deed of gift,
> After his death, of all he dies possessed of.
> (291–93)

Jessica, Lorenzo, and Antonio are thus made happy. Yet, Antonio, restored to wealth but bereft of his friend Bassanio, remains as he was when first rich, "so sad" (I.1.1), and Jessica and Lorenzo, however materially well off, remain a couple of mixed religions subject to the ominous fates they recounted at the act's start.

When Shakespeare named the disguised Portia "Balthasar," many in his audience would have recalled that the Babylonians hostilely renamed the prophet Daniel "Baltassar" (Daniel 1:7) – he/she is thus both prophet (a comic prophet in the play) and alienated. A similar mingling of biblical references occurs at the play's end, when Lorenzo acknowledges Shylock's enforced gift: "Fair ladies, you drop manna in the way / Of starvèd people" (294-95). Manna saved the Israelites in the desert (Exodus 16:14-15) and became a Christian means to salvation (John 6:31-33). At the very end of *The Merchant of Venice,* Shakespeare recalls a word, "manna," Jews and Christians shared, and a biblical moment when Jew and Christian were, or could consider themselves to be, one.

Does this intricate, concluding allusion solve the play's complex social and religious ambiguities? No. Does it solve the play's generic puzzles? No. What does? What might?

A. R. BRAUNMULLER
University of California,
Los Angeles

Note on the Text

THE EARLIEST PREPUBLICATION records refer to this play as "a booke of the Merchaunt of Venyce or otherwise called the Iewe of Venyce" (22 July 1598) and "A booke called the booke of the merchant of Venyce" (28 October 1600). Use of the word "booke" strongly suggests some playhouse associations, since "booke" was the theater's term for the manuscript that regulated performances – i.e., directing entrances and exits, costume changes, sound cues, etc. James Roberts, a printer, and Thomas Heyes, a publisher-bookseller, are mentioned in these records, and together they brought out a quarto (1600): "The most excellent Historie of the *Merchant of Venice* . . . Written by William Shakespeare. . . ." This First Quarto (Q1) later served as the basis for the Second Quarto (Q2), a fraudulent text published in 1619 but claiming publication in 1600, and for the First Folio (F), published in 1623.

The First Quarto is well printed and provides only a few bibliographical problems, of which the most puzzling is the apparent presence in stage directions and speech prefixes of three characters – Salarino, Solanio, Salerio – who could easily be confused, especially if the names were abbreviated, as they often are. Following the analysis in M. M. Mahood's edition (Cambridge: Cambridge University Press, 1987), recent editors have retained three separate speakers rather than combining Salarino and Salerio, as was once the case, and these three appear here. In stage directions and speech prefixes, also, the play's Jewish financier, Shylock, sometimes appears as "Iew[e]" (i.e., Jew, "the Jew"): these occasions have been standardized as "Shylock."

Act divisions first appear in F, and are followed here

along with later, mostly eighteenth-century, editorial divisions into scenes. Further substantive changes from Q1 are listed below, with the adopted reading in italics, followed by the source of that reading (in parentheses) and the Q1 reading, both in roman letters.

I.1 27 *docked* (Rowe) docks   113 *It is that* (Rowe) It is that

II.1 s.d. *Morocco* (Capell) Morochus   31 *thee* (Rowe) the

II.2 3–8 *Gobbo* (Q2) Iobbe

II.7 s.d. *Morocco* (Capell) Morrocho   69 *tombs* (Johnson) timber   77 **s.d.** *Flourish . . . cornets* (Mahood) (appears at opening of next scene in F)

II.8 39 *Slubber* (Q2) slumber

III.1 98 *Heard* (Neilson-Hill) heere

III.2 81 *vice* (F2) voyce   117 *whether* (F) whither

III.3 s.d. *Solanio* (F) Salerio

III.4 49 *Padua* (Theobald) Mantua   50 *cousin's* (F) cosin   53 *traject* (Rowe) Tranect

III.5 20 *e'en* (Q2) in   70–71 *merit it, / In* (Pope) mean it, it   77 *a wife* (F) wife

IV.1 30 *his state* (Q2) this states   31 *flint* (Q2) flints   51 *Master* (Rann) Maisters   74 *bleat* (F) bleake   75 *pines* (F) of Pines   100 *'tis* (Q2) as   208 *thrice* (Dyce) twice   228 *No, not* (Q2) Not not   396 *GRATIANO* (Q2) Shylock

V.1 41–42 *Master Lorenzo? Master Lorenzo!* (Cambridge) M. Lorenzo, & M. Lorenzo   152 *give it you* (Q2) give you

The Merchant of Venice

[Names of the Actors

THE DUKE OF VENICE
THE PRINCE OF MOROCCO ⎫ *Portia's suitors*
THE PRINCE OF ARAGON ⎭
ANTONIO, *a merchant of Venice*
BASSANIO, *his friend, suitor to Portia*
GRATIANO ⎫
SALARINO ⎬ *friends to Antonio and Bassanio*
SOLANIO ⎭
LORENZO
SHYLOCK, *a financier*
TUBAL, *his friend*
LANCELOT GOBBO, *a clown, servant to Shylock*
OLD GOBBO, *father to Lancelot*
LEONARDO, *servant to Bassanio*
BALTHASAR ⎫ *servants to Portia*
STEPHANO ⎭
SALERIO, *a messenger*
PORTIA, *an heiress*
NERISSA, *her waiting gentlewoman*
JESSICA, *Shylock's daughter*
MAGNIFICOES OF VENICE, COURT OFFICERS, JAILER,
    SERVANTS, AND OTHER ATTENDANTS

SCENE: *Venice and Belmont*]
*

The Merchant of Venice

I.1 *Enter Antonio, Salarino, and Solanio.*

ANTONIO
  In sooth I know not why I am so sad.   1
  It wearies me, you say it wearies you;
  But how I caught it, found it, or came by it,
  What stuff 'tis made of, whereof it is born,
  I am to learn;   5
  And such a want-wit sadness makes of me   6
  That I have much ado to know myself.

SALARINO
  Your mind is tossing on the ocean,
  There where your argosies with portly sail –   9
  Like signors and rich burghers on the flood,   10
  Or as it were, the pageants of the sea –   11
  Do overpeer the petty traffickers   12
  That curtsy to them, do them reverence,   13
  As they fly by them with their woven wings.

SOLANIO
  Believe me, sir, had I such venture forth,
  The better part of my affections would
  Be with my hopes abroad. I should be still
  Plucking the grass to know where sits the wind,
  Peering in maps for ports and piers and roads;   19

I.1 A street in Venice **1** *In sooth* truly (Antonio answers a question asked before the dialogue and play begin); *sad* serious, thoughtful **5** *am to learn* have yet to learn **6** *want-wit* (1) dullard, (2) forgetful person **9** *argosies* large merchant ships; *portly* (1) stately, (2) swelling (billowing) **11** *pageants* i.e., like "floats" in a procession **12** *overpeer* tower above **13** *curtsy* bow, dip (i.e., while moving on the waves) **19** *roads* anchorages

20 And every object that might make me fear
Misfortune to my ventures, out of doubt
Would make me sad.

SALARINO   My wind cooling my broth
23 Would blow me to an ague when I thought
What harm a wind too great might do at sea.
I should not see the sandy hourglass run
But I should think of shallows and of flats,
27 And see my wealthy *Andrew* docked in sand,
28 Vailing her high top lower than her ribs
To kiss her burial. Should I go to church
30 And see the holy edifice of stone
And not bethink me straight of dangerous rocks,
Which touching but my gentle vessel's side
33 Would scatter all her spices on the stream,
Enrobe the roaring waters with my silks,
And in a word, but even now worth this,
And now worth nothing? Shall I have the thought
To think on this, and shall I lack the thought
38 That such a thing bechanced would make me sad?
But tell not me: I know Antonio
40 Is sad to think upon his merchandise.

ANTONIO
Believe me, no. I thank my fortune for it
42 My ventures are not in one bottom trusted,
43 Nor to one place; nor is my whole estate
Upon the fortune of this present year.
Therefore my merchandise makes me not sad.

SOLANIO
Why then you are in love.

ANTONIO   Fie, fie!

SOLANIO
Not in love neither? Then let us say you are sad

---

23 *ague* fit of trembling 27 *Andrew* (name of ship) 28 *Vailing* bowing;
high top topmast 33 *spices* (a common cargo from Asia to Venice) 38
bechanced having happened 42 *bottom* ship 43–44 *nor is . . . year* nor is all
my wealth risked at this one time

Because you are not merry; and 'twere as easy
For you to laugh and leap, and say you are merry
Because you are not sad. Now by two-headed Janus,   50
Nature hath framed strange fellows in her time:
Some that will evermore peep through their eyes
And laugh like parrots at a bagpiper,
And other of such vinegar aspect
That they'll not show their teeth in way of smile
Though Nestor swear the jest be laughable.   56
    Enter Bassanio, Lorenzo, and Gratiano.
Here comes Bassanio your most noble kinsman,
Gratiano, and Lorenzo. Fare ye well;
We leave you now with better company.

SALARINO
I would have stayed till I had made you merry,   60
If worthier friends had not prevented me.   61

ANTONIO
Your worth is very dear in my regard.
I take it your own business calls on you,
And you embrace th' occasion to depart.

SALARINO
Good morrow, my good lords.

BASSANIO
Good signors both, when shall we laugh? Say, when?
You grow exceeding strange. Must it be so?   67

SALARINO
We'll make our leisures to attend on yours.   68
               Exeunt Salarino and Solanio.

LORENZO
My Lord Bassanio, since you have found Antonio,
We two will leave you; but at dinnertime   70
I pray you have in mind where we must meet.

---

50 *Janus* Roman god with two faces, one facing the past, the other the future (Shakespeare also thinks [see ll. 52–55] of the classical masks of comedy and tragedy, one smiling, one sad, or *vinegar*)   **56** *Nestor* old and solemn character in the *Iliad*   **61** *prevented* forestalled   **67** *strange* like strangers   **68** *attend on* wait on (i.e., fit)

BASSANIO
I will not fail you.

GRATIANO
You look not well, Signor Antonio.
74   You have too much respect upon the world;
They lose it that do buy it with much care.
Believe me, you are marvelously changed.

ANTONIO
I hold the world but as the world, Gratiano:
A stage where every man must play a part,
And mine a sad one.

GRATIANO   Let me play the fool!
80   With mirth and laughter let old wrinkles come,
81   And let my liver rather heat with wine
82   Than my heart cool with mortifying groans.
Why should a man whose blood is warm within
84   Sit like his grandsire cut in alabaster?
85   Sleep when he wakes? and creep into the jaundice
By being peevish? I tell thee what, Antonio,
I love thee, and 'tis my love that speaks:
88   There are a sort of men whose visages
89   Do cream and mantle like a standing pond,
90   And do a willful stillness entertain
91   With purpose to be dressed in an opinion
92   Of wisdom, gravity, profound conceit,
93   As who should say, "I am Sir Oracle,
And when I ope my lips, let no dog bark!"
O my Antonio, I do know of these
That therefore only are reputed wise
For saying nothing, when I am very sure

---

74 *respect upon* concern for 81 *liver* (to Elizabethans, the seat of the emotions) 82 *mortifying* (1) deadening, (2) penitential 84 *alabaster* stone used for funerary monuments 85 *jaundice* (jaundice was associated with grief, as cause or consequence) 88 *sort* kind, type 89 *cream . . . pond* cover themselves (*mantle*) in scum (*cream*) like a stagnant pool 90 *entertain* take on, assume 91 *opinion* reputation (so also in l. 102) 92 *conceit* thought 93 *Sir Oracle* (the mock title ridicules pretended gravity)

If they should speak would almost damn those ears,   98
Which hearing them would call their brothers fools.
I'll tell thee more of this another time.   100
But fish not with this melancholy bait
For this fool gudgeon, this opinion.   102
Come, good Lorenzo. Fare ye well awhile;
I'll end my exhortation after dinner.

LORENZO
Well, we will leave you then till dinnertime.
I must be one of these same dumb wise men,
For Gratiano never lets me speak.

GRATIANO
Well, keep me company but two years more,
Thou shalt not know the sound of thine own tongue.

ANTONIO
Fare you well; I'll grow a talker for this gear.   110

GRATIANO
Thanks i' faith; for silence is only commendable
In a neat's tongue dried and a maid not vendible.   112

     Exeunt [Gratiano and Lorenzo].

ANTONIO   Is that anything now?

BASSANIO   Gratiano speaks an infinite deal of nothing,
more than any man in all Venice. His reasons are as two
grains of wheat hid in two bushels of chaff: you shall
seek all day ere you find them, and when you have
them they are not worth the search.

ANTONIO
Well, tell me now what lady is the same
To whom you swore a secret pilgrimage,   120
That you today promised to tell me of.

98–99 *If they . . . fools* (See Matthew 5:22: ". . . but whosoever shall say, Thou fool, shall be in danger of hellfire.") **102** *gudgeon* (proverbially, an easily caught fish); *opinion* (compared to a fish not worth catching with cheap bait) **110** *for this gear* because of what you have just said (Antonio implies that by talking he will escape Gratiano's accusation) **112** *neat* ox (the long, thin, and withered tongue is analogous to an impotent old man's penis); *vendible* marketable (i.e., marriageable)

BASSANIO

    'Tis not unknown to you, Antonio,
123 How much I have disabled mine estate
124 By something showing a more swelling port
125 Than my faint means would grant continuance.
126 Nor do I now make moan to be abridged
127 From such a noble rate; but my chief care
    Is to come fairly off from the great debts
    Wherein my time, something too prodigal,
130 Hath left me gaged. To you, Antonio,
    I owe the most in money and in love,
132 And from your love I have a warranty
    To unburden all my plots and purposes
    How to get clear of all the debts I owe.

ANTONIO

    I pray you, good Bassanio, let me know it,
136 And if it stand as you yourself still do,
    Within the eye of honor, be assured
138 My purse, my person, my extremest means
    Lie all unlocked to your occasions.

BASSANIO

140 In my school days, when I had lost one shaft
141 I shot his fellow of the selfsame flight
    The selfsame way, with more advisèd watch
    To find the other forth; and by adventuring both
    I oft found both. I urge this childhood proof
145 Because what follows is pure innocence.
    I owe you much, and like a willful youth
    That which I owe is lost; but if you please

---

123 *disabled* impaired, reduced   124 *something . . . port* somewhat exhibiting a more lavish appearance (i.e., putting up a good "front")   125 *grant continuance* allow to continue   126 *make moan* complain; *abridged* cut down, reduced   127 *noble rate* high scale   130 *gaged* pledged for, owing   132 *from . . . warranty* i.e., my confidence in your love authorizes   136–37 *if . . . honor* if your plan is as honorable as you have always been   138 *person* reputation (as collateral, but an unwittingly literal remark)   140 *shaft* arrow   141 *selfsame* same size and kind   145 *innocence* childlike sincerity, with perhaps a touch of folly

To shoot another arrow that self way
Which you did shoot the first, I do not doubt,
As I will watch the aim, or to find both   150
Or bring your latter hazard back again
And thankfully rest debtor for the first.

ANTONIO

You know me well, and herein spend but time   153
To wind about my love with circumstance;
And out of doubt you do me now more wrong
In making question of my uttermost   156
Than if you had made waste of all I have.
Then do but say to me what I should do
That in your knowledge may by me be done,
And I am prest unto it: therefore speak.   160

BASSANIO

In Belmont is a lady richly left;   161
And she is fair, and fairer than that word,
Of wondrous virtues. Sometimes from her eyes
I did receive fair speechless messages.
Her name is Portia, nothing undervalued   165
To Cato's daughter, Brutus' Portia;   166
Nor is the wide world ignorant of her worth,
For the four winds blow in from every coast
Renownèd suitors, and her sunny locks   169
Hang on her temples like a golden fleece,   170
Which makes her seat of Belmont Colchos' strand,   171
And many Jasons come in quest of her.
O my Antonio, had I but the means
To hold a rival place with one of them,

150–51 *or . . . again* either to discover both arrows (i.e., loans) or return
your second arrow   153–54 *spend . . . circumstance* i.e., needlessly persuade
me with elaborate talk   156 *making . . . uttermost* questioning that I will do
all I can   160 *prest* ready   161 *richly left* rich by inheritance   165–66 *nothing undervalued / To* of no less worth than   166 *Cato's . . . Portia* historically
wife to Brutus, the conspirator against Julius Caesar, and daughter to the
honest Cato Uticensis, a tribune   169 *sunny* i.e., blond (highly valued by
Elizabethan canons of beauty)   170–72 *golden . . . of her* (reference to
Jason's mythical quest for the Golden Fleece)   171 *seat* principal residence;
strand shore

175   I have a mind presages me such thrift
       That I should questionless be fortunate!
ANTONIO
       Thou know'st that all my fortunes are at sea;
178   Neither have I money, nor commodity
       To raise a present sum. Therefore go forth.
180   Try what my credit can in Venice do;
181   That shall be racked even to the uttermost
       To furnish thee to Belmont to fair Portia.
183   Go presently inquire, and so will I,
       Where money is; and I no question make
185   To have it of my trust or for my sake.   *Exeunt.*

*

❧ **I.2** *Enter Portia with her waiting woman, Nerissa.*

1   PORTIA   By my troth, Nerissa, my little body is aweary of
     this great world.
     NERISSA   You would be, sweet madam, if your miseries
     were in the same abundance as your good fortunes are;
     and yet for aught I see, they are as sick that surfeit with
     too much as they that starve with nothing. It is no
7   mean happiness, therefore, to be seated in the mean;
8   superfluity comes sooner by white hairs, but compe-
     tency lives longer.
10   PORTIA   Good sentences, and well pronounced.
     NERISSA   They would be better if well followed.
     PORTIA   If to do were as easy as to know what were good
     to do, chapels had been churches, and poor men's cot-
14   tages princes' palaces. It is a good divine that follows his

---

175 *thrift* (1) profit, (2) thriving 178 *commodity* goods 181 *racked*
stretched, as on the rack 183 *presently* immediately (as throughout the play)
185 *of my trust . . . sake* on the basis of my credit or as a personal favor (cf.
My purse, my person in l. 138)
    I.2 Belmont 1 *troth* faith; *aweary* (Portia's weariness matches Antonio's
sadness in I.1) 7 *mean* small; *seated . . . mean* with neither too much nor
too little (*mean* is a middle way) 8 *comes sooner by* gets sooner 8–9 *compe-
tency* modest means 10 *sentences* maxims, proverbs 14 *divine* preacher

own instructions; I can easier teach twenty what were
good to be done than to be one of the twenty to follow
mine own teaching. The brain may devise laws for the   17
blood, but a hot temper leaps o'er a cold decree; such a 18
hare is madness the youth to skip o'er the meshes of   19
good counsel the cripple. But this reasoning is not in   20
the fashion to choose me a husband. O me, the word
"choose"! I may neither choose who I would nor refuse
who I dislike, so is the will of a living daughter curbed
by the will of a dead father. Is it not hard, Nerissa, that 24
I cannot choose one, nor refuse none?   25

NERISSA Your father was ever virtuous, and holy men at
   their death have good inspirations. Therefore the lottery that he hath devised in these three chests of gold,
   silver, and lead – whereof who chooses his meaning
   chooses you – will no doubt never be chosen by any   30
   rightly but one who you shall rightly love. But what   31
   warmth is there in your affection towards any of these
   princely suitors that are already come?

PORTIA I pray thee overname them, and as thou namest   34
   them I will describe them, and according to my de-   35
   scription level at my affection.   36

NERISSA First, there is the Neapolitan prince.

PORTIA Ay, that's a colt indeed, for he doth nothing but 38
   talk of his horse, and he makes it a great appropriation 39
   to his own good parts that he can shoe him himself. I 40
   am much afeard my lady his mother played false with a 41
   smith.

NERISSA Then is there the County Palatine.   43

17–18 *brain . . . decree* (this contrast between hot emotion and cold reason
reflects Portia's conflict between desire and her father's will: see ll. 20–25)
18 *temper* temperament   19 *meshes* net for catching hares   20 *good counsel*
wisdom   20–21 *not . . . fashion* not the way   24 *will of a dead father* dead father's bequest (with pun on *will* as determination)   25 *refuse none* refuse any
chance at the *lottery* (ll. 27–28)   31 *rightly . . . rightly* correctly . . . truly   34
overname them list their names   34–94 (these lines are a compendium of
Elizabethan stereotypes for foreigners)   36 *level . . . affection* try to decide, or
to guess, how I feel toward them   38 *colt* raw adolescent   39 *appropriation*
addition   40 *parts* abilities   41 *afeard* afraid   43 *County* count

PORTIA   He doth nothing but frown – as who should say,
45   "An you will not have me, choose!" He hears merry
tales and smiles not; I fear he will prove the weeping
philosopher when he grows old, being so full of un-
mannerly sadness in his youth. I had rather be married
to a death's-head with a bone in his mouth than to ei-
50   ther of these. God defend me from these two!

NERISSA   How say you by the French lord, Monsieur Le
Bon?

PORTIA   God made him, and therefore let him pass for a
man. In truth, I know it is a sin to be a mocker, but
he – why he hath a horse better than the Neapolitan's, a
better bad habit of frowning than the Count Palatine:
57   he is every man in no man. If a throstle sing, he falls
straight a-capering; he will fence with his own shadow.
If I should marry him, I should marry twenty hus-
60   bands. If he would despise me, I would forgive him; for
if he love me to madness, I shall never requite him.

NERISSA   What say you then to Falconbridge, the young
baron of England?

PORTIA   You know I say nothing to him, for he understands not me, nor I him. He hath neither Latin, French,
nor Italian, and you will come into the court and swear
that I have a poor pennyworth in the English. He is a
68   proper man's picture, but alas who can converse with a
69   dumb show? How oddly he is suited! I think he bought
70   his doublet in Italy, his round hose in France, his bonnet
in Germany, and his behavior everywhere.

NERISSA   What think you of the Scottish lord, his neigh-
bor?

PORTIA   That he hath a neighborly charity in him, for he
borrowed a box of the ear of the Englishman and swore

---

45 *An* if; *choose* have it your way (i.e., choose whom you will)   **57** *every . . .
man* everyone in no one; *throstle* thrush   **68** *proper* handsome   **69** *dumb
show* pantomime; *suited* dressed (ll. 69–71 ridicule English aping of other
nations' fashions and customs)   **70** *doublet* coat; *hose* breeches

he would pay him again when he was able. I think the
Frenchman became his surety and sealed under for an-　77
other.

NERISSA　How like you the young German, the Duke of
Saxony's nephew?　　80

PORTIA　Very vilely in the morning when he is sober, and
most vilely in the afternoon when he is drunk. When
he is best he is a little worse than a man, and when he is
worst he is little better than a beast. And the worst fall　84
that ever fell, I hope I shall make shift to go without　85
him.

NERISSA　If he should offer to choose, and choose the
right casket, you should refuse to perform your father's
will if you should refuse to accept him.

PORTIA　Therefore, for fear of the worst, I pray thee set a　90
deep glass of Rhenish wine on the contrary casket, for if　91
the devil be within and that temptation without, I
know he will choose it. I will do anything, Nerissa, ere
I will be married to a sponge.

NERISSA　You need not fear, lady, the having any of these
lords. They have acquainted me with their determina-
tions, which is indeed to return to their home and to
trouble you with no more suit, unless you may be won
by some other sort than your father's imposition, de-　99
pending on the caskets.　　100

PORTIA　If I live to be as old as Sibylla, I will die as chaste　101
as Diana unless I be obtained by the manner of my fa-　102
ther's will. I am glad this parcel of wooers are so reasonable, for there is not one among them but I dote on his
very absence; and I pray God grant them a fair depar-
ture.

---

77 *became his surety* (a reference to the historical Franco-Scottish alliance
against England); *sealed under* put his seal under the Scot's, as a further guarantor (a comic parallel to the Antonio-Bassanio relation)　84 *And* if　85
make shift manage　91 *contrary* other, or "wrong"　99 *sort* way　101 *Sibylla*
prophetess to whom Apollo promised as many years of life as there were
grains in her handful of sand　102 *Diana* goddess of chastity

NERISSA   Do you not remember, lady, in your father's time, a Venetian, a scholar and a soldier, that came hither in the company of the Marquis of Montferrat?

110   PORTIA   Yes, yes, it was Bassanio – as I think, so was he called.

NERISSA   True, madam. He, of all the men that ever my foolish eyes looked upon, was the best deserving a fair lady.

PORTIA   I remember him well, and I remember him worthy of thy praise.

Enter a Servingman.

How now, what news?

SERVINGMAN   The four strangers seek for you, madam, to take their leave, and there is a forerunner come from

120   a fifth, the Prince of Morocco, who brings word the prince his master will be here tonight.

PORTIA   If I could bid the fifth welcome with so good heart as I can bid the other four farewell, I should be

124   glad of his approach. If he have the condition of a saint and the complexion of a devil, I had rather he should

126   shrive me than wive me. Come, Nerissa. Sirrah, go before. Whiles we shut the gate upon one wooer, another knocks at the door.   *Exeunt.*

*

～ I.3   *Enter Bassanio with Shylock the Jew.*

1   SHYLOCK   Three thousand ducats – well.

BASSANIO   Ay, sir, for three months.

SHYLOCK   For three months – well.

124–26 *If . . . wive me* i.e., if his inner nature (*condition*) is saintly and his outer appearance (*complexion*) devilish, I'd want him to hear my confession (*shrive me*) rather than marry me (but note the implicit racism, since Elizabethans often regarded Moroccans as "black," supposedly the devil's skin color)   126 *Sirrah* (form of address to servants)

I.3 Venice   1 *ducats* gold coins (3,000 ducats was a very large sum; later a diamond is valued at 2,000 ducats: see III.1.77–78)

BASSANIO   For the which, as I told you, Antonio shall be
bound.   5

SHYLOCK   Antonio shall become bound – well.

BASSANIO   May you stead me? Will you pleasure me?   7
Shall I know your answer?

SHYLOCK   Three thousand ducats for three months, and
Antonio bound.   10

BASSANIO   Your answer to that.

SHYLOCK   Antonio is a good man.   12

BASSANIO   Have you heard any imputation to the contrary?

SHYLOCK   Ho no, no, no, no! My meaning in saying he
is a good man is to have you understand me that he is
sufficient. Yet his means are in supposition. He hath an   17
argosy bound to Tripolis, another to the Indies; I understand, moreover, upon the Rialto, he hath a third at   19
Mexico, a fourth for England, and other ventures he   20
hath squandered abroad. But ships are but boards,   21
sailors but men; there be land rats and water rats, water
thieves and land thieves – I mean pirates; and then
there is the peril of waters, winds, and rocks. The man
is, notwithstanding, sufficient. Three thousand ducats –
I think I may take his bond.

BASSANIO   Be assured you may.

SHYLOCK   I will be assured I may; and that I may be assured, I will bethink me. May I speak with Antonio?

BASSANIO   If it please you to dine with us.   30

SHYLOCK   Yes, to smell pork, to eat of the habitation   31
which your prophet the Nazarite conjured the devil   32
into! I will buy with you, sell with you, talk with you,

---

5 *bound* responsible, as a surety   7 *stead* accommodate   12 *good* reliable in
business dealings   17 *sufficient* good as a guarantor; *in supposition* uncertain
19 *Rialto* area of the Venetian Exchange (i.e., "stock exchange" or "bourse")
21 *squandered* scattered (but with a hint of foolish financial speculation)   31
habitation body   32–33 *Nazarite . . . into* (reference to Jesus' [*the Nazarite*]
casting of evil spirits into a herd of swine; see Luke 8:26–33, Mark 5:1–13,
Matthew 8:28–32)

walk with you, and so following; but I will not eat with
35   you, drink with you, nor pray with you. What news on
the Rialto? Who is he comes here?
> *Enter Antonio.*

BASSANIO
  This is Signor Antonio.

SHYLOCK   *[Aside]*
38   How like a fawning publican he looks.
39   I hate him for he is a Christian;
40   But more, for that in low simplicity
  He lends out money gratis and brings down
42   The rate of usance here with us in Venice.
43   If I can catch him once upon the hip,
  I will feed fat the ancient grudge I bear him.
  He hates our sacred nation, and he rails,
  Even there where merchants most do congregate,
  On me, my bargains, and my well-won thrift,
  Which he calls interest. Cursèd be my tribe
  If I forgive him.

BASSANIO   Shylock, do you hear?

SHYLOCK
50   I am debating of my present store,
  And by the near guess of my memory
52   I cannot instantly raise up the gross
  Of full three thousand ducats. What of that?
  Tubal, a wealthy Hebrew of my tribe,
  Will furnish me. But soft, how many months
  Do you desire? *[To Antonio]* Rest you fair, good signor!
  Your worship was the last man in our mouths.

ANTONIO
  Shylock, albeit I neither lend nor borrow
59   By taking nor by giving of excess,

35–36 *What . . . Rialto* (Shylock changes the subject) 38 *publican* tax col-
lector (see Luke 18:9–14, where the humble *publican* is contrasted with the
arrogant Pharisee – the allusion works against Shylock's hostility) 39 *for* because 42 *usance* interest 43 *catch . . . hip* i.e., get him in a weak position
(figure of speech from wrestling) 50 *store* wealth 52 *gross* full amount 59
excess interest

Yet to supply the ripe wants of my friend   60
I'll break a custom. *[To Bassanio]* Is he yet possessed   61
How much ye would?

SHYLOCK   Ay, ay, three thousand ducats.

ANTONIO
And for three months.

SHYLOCK
I had forgot – three months, you told me so.
Well then, your bond. And let me see – but hear you,   65
Methoughts you said you neither lend nor borrow   66
Upon advantage.

ANTONIO   I do never use it.

SHYLOCK
When Jacob grazed his uncle Laban's sheep –   68
This Jacob from our holy Abram was,
As his wise mother wrought in his behalf,   70
The third possessor; ay, he was the third –   71

ANTONIO
And what of him? Did he take interest?

SHYLOCK
No, not take interest – not as you would say
Directly interest. Mark what Jacob did:
When Laban and himself were compromised   75
That all the eanlings which were streaked and pied   76
Should fall as Jacob's hire, the ewes being rank   77
In end of autumn turnèd to the rams;
And when the work of generation was
Between these woolly breeders in the act,   80
The skillful shepherd peeled me certain wands,   81

---

60 *ripe* immediate   61–62 *possessed . . . would* informed of how much you
want   65 *but hear you* (equivalent to "wait a minute")   66 *Methoughts* it
seemed to me   68 *Jacob* (see Genesis 27 and 30:25–43)   71 *third possessor*
i.e., of the birthright descending from his grandfather Abraham   75 *compromised* agreed   76 *eanlings* lambs; *pied* spotted   77 *hire* share, recompense;
rank in heat   81–85 *peeled . . . parti-colored* (Jacob's success depends on the
now outmoded theory of prenatal influence: here the variegated *wands* in-
duce variegated *lambs*)   81 *peeled me* peeled (*me* is Shylock's colloquial way
of asserting the story's importance to him); *wands* branches, shoots

82 And in the doing of the deed of kind
83 He stuck them up before the fulsome ewes,
84 Who then conceiving, did in eaning time
85 Fall parti-colored lambs, and those were Jacob's.
    This was a way to thrive, and he was blessed;
87 And thrift is blessing if men steal it not.

ANTONIO
88 This was a venture, sir, that Jacob served for,
   A thing not in his power to bring to pass,
90 But swayed and fashioned by the hand of heaven.
91 Was this inserted to make interest good?
92 Or is your gold and silver ewes and rams?

SHYLOCK
   I cannot tell; I make it breed as fast.
   But note me, signor –

ANTONIO   Mark you this, Bassanio,
   The devil can cite Scripture for his purpose.
   An evil soul producing holy witness
   Is like a villain with a smiling cheek,
   A goodly apple rotten at the heart.
   O what a goodly outside falsehood hath!

SHYLOCK
100 Three thousand ducats – 'tis a good round sum.
    Three months from twelve – then let me see, the rate –

ANTONIO
102 Well, Shylock, shall we be beholding to you?

SHYLOCK
    Signor Antonio, many a time and oft
104 In the Rialto you have rated me
    About my moneys and my usances.

---

82 *kind* nature 83 *fulsome* lustful (?) 84 *eaning* lambing 85 *Fall* drop, give birth to 87 *thrift* (etymologically derived from *thrive*) 88–89 *venture . . . pass* i.e., a commercial venture of some uncertainty 91 *inserted . . . good* brought in to justify charging interest 92 *gold . . . rams* (a main Elizabethan argument against usury was that it blasphemously caused inanimate metal to multiply as living creatures did at God's command; see Genesis 8:17 and 9:1) 102 *beholding* in debt 104 *rated* railed at, reviled

Still have I borne it with a patient shrug,
For suff'rance is the badge of all our tribe.   107
You call me misbeliever, cutthroat dog,
And spit upon my Jewish gaberdine,   109
And all for use of that which is mine own.   110
Well then, it now appears you need my help.
Go to then. You come to me and you say,   112
"Shylock, we would have moneys" – you say so,
You that did void your rheum upon my beard   114
And foot me as you spurn a stranger cur
Over your threshold: moneys is your suit.
What should I say to you? Should I not say,
"Hath a dog money? Is it possible
A cur can lend three thousand ducats?" Or
Shall I bend low, and in a bondman's key,   120
With bated breath and whisp'ring humbleness,
Say this:
"Fair sir, you spit on me on Wednesday last,
You spurned me such a day, another time
You called me dog; and for these courtesies
I'll lend you thus much moneys."

ANTONIO
I am as like to call thee so again,
To spit on thee again, to spurn thee too.
If thou wilt lend this money, lend it not
As to thy friends, for when did friendship take   130
A breed for barren metal of his friend?   131
But lend it rather to thine enemy,
Who if he break, thou mayst with better face   133
Exact the penalty.

SHYLOCK   Why look you, how you storm!
I would be friends with you and have your love,

---

107 *suff'rance* forbearance, endurance; *badge* distinctive mark (the word can
specifically mean a metal or cloth emblem worn to indicate one's master's
family or, in Renaissance Venice, one's Judaism) 109 *gaberdine* cloak 112
Go to (exclamation of impatience, like "Come, come!") 114 *rheum* spittle
131 *A . . . friend* (see note to l. 92, above) 133 *break* goes bankrupt

Forget the shames that you have stained me with,
137 Supply your present wants, and take no doit
Of usance for my moneys, and you'll not hear me.
139 This is kind I offer.

BASSANIO
140 This were kindness.

SHYLOCK
This kindness will I show:
Go with me to a notary; seal me there
143 Your single bond, and – in a merry sport –
If you repay me not on such a day,
In such a place, such sum or sums as are
Expressed in the condition, let the forfeit
147 Be nominated for an equal pound
Of your fair flesh, to be cut off and taken
In what part of your body pleaseth me.

ANTONIO
150 Content, in faith. I'll seal to such a bond,
And say there is much kindness in the Jew.

BASSANIO
You shall not seal to such a bond for me!
153 I'll rather dwell in my necessity.

ANTONIO
Why fear not, man; I will not forfeit it.
Within these two months – that's a month before
This bond expires – I do expect return
Of thrice three times the value of this bond.

SHYLOCK
O father Abram, what these Christians are,
Whose own hard dealings teaches them suspect
160 The thoughts of others! Pray you tell me this:
161 If he should break his day, what should I gain

---

137 *doit* coin of very small value   139 *kind I offer* i.e., a kindly offer (with a suggestion of "natural" dealing; Antonio has called usury unnatural)   143 *single* without other security; *in . . . sport* i.e., as a jesting penalty (but flesh is *kind,* "natural," which Shylock said he offered)   147 *nominated* named, prescribed; *equal* exact   153 *dwell . . . necessity* i.e., remain in need   161 *break his day* fail to pay on the due date

By the exaction of the forfeiture?
A pound of man's flesh taken from a man
Is not so estimable, profitable neither,
As flesh of muttons, beefs, or goats. I say
To buy his favor I extend this friendship.
If he will take it, so; if not, adieu.
And for my love I pray you wrong me not.

ANTONIO
Yes, Shylock, I will seal unto this bond.   169

SHYLOCK
Then meet me forthwith at the notary's;   *170*
Give him direction for this merry bond,
And I will go and purse the ducats straight,   172
See to my house, left in the fearful guard   173
Of an unthrifty knave, and presently   174
I'll be with you.   *Exit.*   175

ANTONIO   Hie thee, gentle Jew.
The Hebrew will turn Christian; he grows kind.

BASSANIO
I like not fair terms and a villain's mind.

ANTONIO
Come on. In this there can be no dismay;
My ships come home a month before the day.   *Exeunt.*

*

∿ II.1 *[Flourish of cornets.] Enter [the Prince of] Mo-*
    rocco, a tawny Moor all in white, and three or four fol-
    lowers accordingly, with Portia, Nerissa, and their train.

MOROCCO
Mislike me not for my complexion,

---

169 *Yes ... bond* (Antonio does not respond to Shylock's preceding line)
172 *purse* procure, gather   173 *fearful* (1) timorous, (2) to be feared (hence
suspected)   174 *unthrifty* careless, extravagant   175 *gentle* (with pun on
"gentile"?)
    II.1 Portia's house, Belmont s.d. *Flourish* distinctive melody introducing
important persons; *tawny* (often used by Elizabethans to describe the skin
color of North Africans); *accordingly* i.e., the followers are made up and
dressed as Morocco is

2   The shadowed livery of the burnished sun,
     To whom I am a neighbor and near bred.
     Bring me the fairest creature northward born,
5   Where Phoebus' fire scarce thaws the icicles,
6   And let us make incision for your love
     To prove whose blood is reddest, his or mine.
8   I tell thee, lady, this aspect of mine
9   Hath feared the valiant. By my love I swear
10   The best-regarded virgins of our clime
     Have loved it too. I would not change this hue,
12   Except to steal your thoughts, my gentle queen.

PORTIA
13   In terms of choice I am not solely led
14   By nice direction of a maiden's eyes.
     Besides, the lott'ry of my destiny
     Bars me the right of voluntary choosing.
17   But if my father had not scanted me,
     And hedged me by his wit to yield myself
     His wife who wins me by that means I told you,
20   Yourself, renownèd prince, then stood as fair
     As any comer I have looked on yet
     For my affection.

MOROCCO   Even for that I thank you.
     Therefore I pray you lead me to the caskets
     To try my fortune. By this scimitar,
25   That slew the Sophy and a Persian prince
26   That won three fields of Sultan Solyman,
27   I would o'erstare the sternest eyes that look,
     Outbrave the heart most daring on the earth,
     Pluck the young sucking cubs from the she-bear,

---

2 *shadowed . . . sun* darkened official garb of the sun's retainers (i.e., dark skin)   5 *Phoebus* the sun   6 *make incision* cut to draw blood   8 *aspect* countenance   9 *feared* frightened   12 *steal your thoughts* i.e., win your favor   13 *terms* matters   14 *nice* fastidious   17 *scanted* restricted   25 *Sophy* Shah of Persia   26 *Solyman* a Turkish ruler   27 *o'erstare* outstare

Yea, mock the lion when a roars for prey,   30
To win thee, lady. But alas the while,
If Hercules and Lichas play at dice   32
Which is the better man, the greater throw
May turn by fortune from the weaker hand.
So is Alcides beaten by his rogue,   35
And so may I, blind Fortune leading me,
Miss that which one unworthier may attain,
And die with grieving.

PORTIA   You must take your chance,
And either not attempt to choose at all
Or swear before you choose, if you choose wrong   40
Never to speak to lady afterward
In way of marriage. Therefore be advised.   42

MOROCCO
Nor will not. Come, bring me unto my chance.   43

PORTIA
First, forward to the temple; after dinner   44
Your hazard shall be made.

MOROCCO   Good fortune then,
To make me blessed or cursèd'st among men!

                    [Flourish of cornets.] Exeunt.

                              *

∾ **II.2** *Enter [Lancelot Gobbo] the Clown, alone.*

LANCELOT   Certainly my conscience will serve me to run
from this Jew my master. The fiend is at mine elbow
and tempts me, saying to me, "Gobbo, Lancelot
Gobbo, good Lancelot," or "good Gobbo," or "good
Lancelot Gobbo – use your legs, take the start, run

---

30 *a* he   **32** *Lichas* servant of Hercules (Lichas unwittingly gave Hercules a
poisoned shirt, which drove him to madness and death)   **35** *Alcides* Hercules   **42** *be advised* consider, reflect   **43** *Nor will not* i.e., I agree to the conditions just imposed   **44** *to the temple* i.e., to swear the oath
    II.2 A street in Venice

away." My conscience says, "No. Take heed, honest
Lancelot; take heed, honest Gobbo," or as aforesaid,
8   "honest Lancelot Gobbo; do not run, scorn running
with thy heels." Well, the most courageous fiend bids
10   me pack. "Fia!" says the fiend; "away!" says the fiend.
11   "For the heavens, rouse up a brave mind," says the
fiend, "and run." Well, my conscience hanging about
the neck of my heart says very wisely to me, "My honest friend Lancelot, being an honest man's son," or
rather "an honest woman's son," for indeed my father
16   did something smack, something grow to; he had a
kind of taste: Well, my conscience says, "Lancelot,
budge not." "Budge," says the fiend. "Budge not," says
my conscience. "Conscience," say I, "you counsel
20   well." "Fiend," say I, "you counsel well." To be ruled by
my conscience, I should stay with the Jew my master
22   who, God bless the mark, is a kind of devil; and to run
away from the Jew, I should be ruled by the fiend, who,
24   saving your reverence, is the devil himself. Certainly
25   the Jew is the very devil incarnation; and in my conscience, my conscience is but a kind of hard conscience
to offer to counsel me to stay with the Jew. The fiend
gives the more friendly counsel. I will run, fiend; my
heels are at your commandment; I will run.

Enter Old Gobbo with a basket.

30   GOBBO   Master young man, you, I pray you, which is the
way to Master Jew's?

8–9 *scorn . . . heels* reject, despise (with pun on "kick at")   10 *pack* be off;
Fia away (Italian *via*)   11 *For the heavens* for heaven's sake   16–17
smack . . . grow to . . . taste kiss noisily . . . have an erection . . . leaning, en-
joyment (i.e., Gobbo's father was promiscuous, not *honest*)   22, 24 *God . . .
mark, saving . . . reverence* (conventional phrases of apology for what one is
about to say)   25 *incarnation* i.e., incarnate (Gobbo's error comes close to
identifying devil and Christ)

LANCELOT   *[Aside]* O heavens, this is my true-begotten
father who, being more than sand-blind, high-gravel-   33
blind, knows me not. I will try confusions with him.   34

GOBBO   Master young gentleman, I pray you which is
the way to Master Jew's?

LANCELOT   Turn up on your right hand at the next turning, but at the next turning of all, on your left; marry,   38
at the very next turning turn of no hand, but turn
down indirectly to the Jew's house.   40

GOBBO   Be God's sonties, 'twill be a hard way to hit! Can   41
you tell me whether one Lancelot that dwells with him,
dwell with him or no?

LANCELOT   Talk you of young Master Lancelot? *[Aside]*   44
Mark me now; now will I raise the waters. – Talk you   45
of young Master Lancelot?

GOBBO   No master, sir, but a poor man's son. His father,
though I say't, is an honest exceeding poor man and,
God be thanked, well to live.   49

LANCELOT   Well, let his father be what a will, we talk of   50
young Master Lancelot.

GOBBO   Your worship's friend, and Lancelot, sir.

LANCELOT   But I pray you, ergo old man, ergo I beseech   53
you, talk you of young Master Lancelot?

GOBBO   Of Lancelot, an't please your mastership.

LANCELOT   Ergo, Master Lancelot. Talk not of Master
Lancelot, father, for the young gentleman, according to
fates and destinies and such odd sayings, the Sisters   58
Three and such branches of learning, is indeed deceased,
or as you would say in plain terms, gone to heaven.   60

GOBBO   Marry, God forbid! The boy was the very staff of
my age, my very prop.

---

33 *sand-blind* half blind   33–34 *high-gravel-blind* blinder than *sand-blind*
34 *try confusions* (wordplay on "try conclusions" – to experiment)   38 *marry*
to be sure (an interjection)   41 *Be* by; *sonties* saints (?), sanctities (?)   44
Master (title applied to young gentlemen)   45 *raise the waters* i.e., start
something (raise tears?)   49 *well to live* well-to-do   53 *ergo* therefore (Latin)
58–59 *Sisters Three* the three Fates

63 LANCELOT Do I look like a cudgel or a hovel post, a staff or a prop? Do you know me, father?

GOBBO Alack the day, I know you not, young gentle-man, but I pray you tell me, is my boy, God rest his soul, alive or dead?

LANCELOT Do you not know me, father?

GOBBO Alack, sir, I am sand-blind! I know you not.

70 LANCELOT Nay, indeed if you had your eyes you might
71 fail of the knowing me; it is a wise father that knows his own child. Well, old man, I will tell you news of your son. *[Kneels.]* Give me your blessing. Truth will come to light; murder cannot be hid long, a man's son may, but in the end truth will out.

GOBBO Pray you, sir, stand up. I am sure you are not Lancelot my boy.

LANCELOT Pray you let's have no more fooling about it, but give me your blessing. I am Lancelot – your boy
80 that was, your son that is, your child that shall be.

GOBBO I cannot think you are my son.

LANCELOT I know not what I shall think of that, but I am Lancelot, the Jew's man, and I am sure Margery your wife is my mother.

GOBBO Her name is Margery indeed! I'll be sworn, if thou be Lancelot thou art mine own flesh and blood.
87 Lord worshiped might he be, what a beard hast thou got! Thou hast got more hair on thy chin than Dobbin
89 my fill horse has on his tail.

90 LANCELOT *[Rises.]* It should seem then that Dobbin's tail grows backward. I am sure he had more hair of his tail than I have of my face when I last saw him.

GOBBO Lord, how art thou changed! How dost thou and thy master agree? I have brought him a present. How 'gree you now?

---

63 *hovel post* timber supporting a shack   **71–72** *wise . . . child* (proverb that recalls old Gobbo's dishonest reputation, ll. 14–17)   **87** *beard* (apparently Gobbo has placed his hand on the back of Lancelot's head)   **89** *fill horse* cart horse

LANCELOT   Well, well; but for mine own part, as I have
set up my rest to run away, so I will not rest till I have   97
run some ground. My master's a very Jew. Give him a   98
present? Give him a halter! I am famished in his service;   99
you may tell every finger I have with my ribs. Father, I   100
am glad you are come. Give me your present to one
Master Bassanio, who indeed gives rare new liveries. If I   102
serve not him, I will run as far as God has any ground.
O rare fortune, here comes the man! To him, father, for
I am a Jew if I serve the Jew any longer.
    Enter Bassanio, with [Leonardo and] a follower or
    two.

BASSANIO   You may do so, but let it be so hasted that
supper be ready at the farthest by five of the clock. See
these letters delivered, put the liveries to making, and
desire Gratiano to come anon to my lodging.   109
    [Exit one of his men.]

LANCELOT   To him, father!   *110*

GOBBO   God bless your worship!

BASSANIO   Gramercy. Wouldst thou aught with me?   112

GOBBO   Here's my son, sir, a poor boy –

LANCELOT   Not a poor boy, sir, but the rich Jew's man
that would, sir, as my father shall specify –

GOBBO   He hath a great infection, sir, as one would say,   116
to serve –

LANCELOT   Indeed, the short and the long is, I serve the
Jew, and have a desire, as my father shall specify –

GOBBO   His master and he, saving your worship's rever-   *120*
ence, are scarce cater-cousins.   *121*

LANCELOT   To be brief, the very truth is that the Jew having done me wrong doth cause me, as my father, being
I hope an old man, shall frutify unto you –   *124*

---

97 *set . . . rest* i.e., determined **98** *very* complete, entire (an intensive) **99**
halter hangman's noose **100** *tell* count **102** *liveries* costumes for servants
109 *anon* presently, at once **112** *Gramercy* many thanks **116** *infection* i.e.,
"affection" **121** *cater-cousins* close friends **124** *frutify* i.e., "fructify"

GOBBO   I have here a dish of doves that I would bestow
upon your worship, and my suit is –

127 LANCELOT   In very brief, the suit is impertinent to myself, as your worship shall know by this honest old man,
and though I say it, though old man, yet poor man, my

130 father –

BASSANIO   One speak for both. What would you?

LANCELOT   Serve you, sir.

133 GOBBO   That is the very defect of the matter, sir.

BASSANIO

I know thee well; thou hast obtained thy suit.
Shylock thy master spoke with me this day,

136 And hath preferred thee, if it be preferment
To leave a rich Jew's service to become
The follower of so poor a gentleman.

139 LANCELOT   The old proverb is very well parted between
140 my master Shylock and you, sir. You have the grace of
God, sir, and he hath enough.

BASSANIO

Thou speak'st it well. Go, father, with thy son;
Take leave of thy old master and inquire
My lodging out. *[To a follower]* Give him a livery

145 More guarded than his fellows'. See it done.

LANCELOT   Father, in. I cannot get a service; no! I have
ne'er a tongue in my head; well! *[Looks at his palm.]* If

148 any man in Italy have a fairer table which doth offer to
swear upon a book – I shall have good fortune! Go to,

150 here's a simple line of life. Here's a small trifle of wives!
Alas, fifteen wives is nothing; eleven widows and nine

152 maids is a simple coming-in for one man. And then to

153 scape drowning thrice, and to be in peril of my life with

---

127 *impertinent* i.e., "pertinent"   133 *defect* i.e., "effect"   136 *preferred* rec-
ommended for advancement   139–41 *proverb . . . enough* (play on the
proverb "He who has the grace of God has enough")   145 *guarded* deco-
rated with braid   148 *table* palm of hand (Lancelot now "reads" the lines of
his palm)   152 *simple coming-in* just a start (with wordplay on "coming in"
women)   153, 154 *scape, scapes* escape, escapes   153–54 *peril . . . feather
bed* i.e., endangered by an angry cuckolded spouse (?) (*feather bed* seems to
mean [someone else's] marriage bed)

the edge of a feather bed! Here are simple scapes. Well,   154
if Fortune be a woman, she's a good wench for this gear.   155
Father, come. I'll take my leave of the Jew in the twin-
kling.   *Exit Clown [Lancelot, with Old Gobbo].*

BASSANIO
    I pray thee, good Leonardo, think on this:
    These things being bought and orderly bestowed,
    Return in haste, for I do feast tonight   160
    My best esteemed acquaintance. Hie thee, go.

LEONARDO
    My best endeavors shall be done herein.
        Enter Gratiano.

GRATIANO
    Where's your master?

LEONARDO   Yonder, sir, he walks.   *[Exit.]*

GRATIANO
    Signor Bassanio!

BASSANIO   Gratiano?

GRATIANO
    I have suit to you.

BASSANIO   You have obtained it.

GRATIANO   You must not deny me. I must go with you
    to Belmont.

BASSANIO
    Why then you must. But hear thee, Gratiano:
    Thou art too wild, too rude, and bold of voice –
    Parts that become thee happily enough   170
    And in such eyes as ours appear not faults;
    But where thou art not known, why there they show
    Something too liberal. Pray thee take pain   173
    To allay with some cold drops of modesty   174
    Thy skipping spirit, lest through thy wild behavior
    I be misconstered in the place I go to,   176
    And lose my hopes.

---

155 *this gear* these matters   **170** *Parts* qualities   **173** *liberal* free   **174** *modesty* expected behavior   **176** *misconstered* misunderstood

GRATIANO   Signor Bassanio, hear me:
178   If I do not put on a sober habit,
       Talk with respect, and swear but now and then,
180   Wear prayer books in my pocket, look demurely,
181   Nay more, while grace is saying hood mine eyes
       Thus with my hat, and sigh and say "amen,"
183   Use all the observance of civility
184   Like one well studied in a sad ostent
       To please his grandam, never trust me more.

BASSANIO
       Well, we shall see your bearing.

GRATIANO
187   Nay, but I bar tonight. You shall not gauge me
       By what we do tonight.

BASSANIO   No, that were pity.
       I would entreat you rather to put on
190   Your boldest suit of mirth, for we have friends
       That purpose merriment. But fare you well;
       I have some business.

GRATIANO
       And I must to Lorenzo and the rest,
       But we will visit you at suppertime.   *Exeunt.*

                          *

~ **II.3** *Enter Jessica and [Lancelot] the Clown.*

JESSICA
       I am sorry thou wilt leave my father so;
       Our house is hell, and thou a merry devil
       Didst rob it of some taste of tediousness.
       But fare thee well; there is a ducat for thee.
       And, Lancelot, soon at supper shalt thou see
       Lorenzo, who is thy new master's guest.
       Give him this letter; do it secretly.

---

178 *habit* (1) garb, (2) demeanor 181 *hood* cover 183 *civility* polite behavior 184 *sad ostent* solemn appearance 187 *gauge* measure, judge
   II.3 Shylock's house

And so farewell; I would not have my father
See me in talk with thee.

LANCELOT   Adieu! Tears exhibit my tongue. Most beauti- 10
ful pagan, most sweet Jew! If a Christian do not play 11
the knave and get thee, I am much deceived. But adieu! 12
These foolish drops do something drown my manly
spirit. Adieu!

JESSICA
Farewell, good Lancelot.   *[Exit Lancelot.]*
Alack, what heinous sin is it in me   16
To be ashamed to be my father's child.
But though I am a daughter to his blood,
I am not to his manners. O Lorenzo,
If thou keep promise, I shall end this strife,   20
Become a Christian and thy loving wife!   *Exit.*

                                    *

❧ **II.4** *Enter Gratiano, Lorenzo, Salarino, and Solanio.*

LORENZO
Nay, we will slink away in suppertime,   1
Disguise us at my lodging, and return
All in an hour.

GRATIANO
We have not made good preparation.

SALARINO
We have not spoke us yet of torchbearers.   5

SOLANIO
'Tis vile, unless it may be quaintly ordered,   6
And better in my mind not undertook.

LORENZO
'Tis now but four of clock. We have two hours
To furnish us.

---

10 *exhibit* i.e., inhibit (but also: "tears say what my tongue cannot")   **11–12**
If . . . thee (cf. ll. 17–18)   **12** *get* beget   **16** *sin* i.e., Jessica breaks the Fourth
Commandment
    II.4 A public place   **1** *slink away* get away unnoticed   **5** *spoke . . . torch-*
bearers ordered torchbearers   **6** *quaintly ordered* nicely, or elaborately,
arranged

Enter Lancelot [with a letter].

Friend Lancelot, what's the news?

10 LANCELOT An it shall please you to break up this, it shall
seem to signify.

LORENZO
I know the hand. In faith, 'tis a fair hand,
And whiter than the paper it writ on
Is the fair hand that writ.

GRATIANO   Love news, in faith!

LANCELOT By your leave, sir.

LORENZO Whither goest thou?

LANCELOT Marry, sir, to bid my old master the Jew to
sup tonight with my new master the Christian.

LORENZO
Hold here, take this. *[Gives money.]* Tell gentle Jessica
20 I will not fail her. Speak it privately.

Exit Clown [Lancelot].

Go, gentlemen:
Will you prepare you for this masque tonight?
I am provided of a torchbearer.

SALARINO
24 Ay, marry, I'll be gone about it straight.

SOLANIO
And so will I.

LORENZO   Meet me and Gratiano
At Gratiano's lodging some hour hence.

SALARINO
'Tis good we do so.   *Exit [with Solanio].*

GRATIANO
Was not that letter from fair Jessica?

LORENZO
I must needs tell thee all. She hath directed
30 How I shall take her from her father's house,
What gold and jewels she is furnished with,
What page's suit she hath in readiness.
If e'er the Jew her father come to heaven,

---

10 *break up* break open   24 *straight* right away

It will be for his gentle daughter's sake;   34
And never dare misfortune cross her foot,   35
Unless she do it under this excuse,   36
That she is issue to a faithless Jew.   37
Come, go with me; peruse this as thou goest.
Fair Jessica shall be my torchbearer.

                     Exit [with Gratiano].

              *

II.5   *Enter [Shylock the] Jew and [Lancelot,] his man
that was, the Clown.*

SHYLOCK
Well, thou shalt see, thy eyes shall be thy judge,
The difference of old Shylock and Bassanio –   2
What, Jessica! – Thou shalt not gormandize
As thou hast done with me – What, Jessica! –
And sleep, and snore, and rend apparel out –   5
Why, Jessica, I say!
LANCELOT   Why, Jessica!
SHYLOCK
Who bids thee call? I do not bid thee call.
LANCELOT   Your worship was wont to tell me I could do
nothing without bidding.
     Enter Jessica.
JESSICA   Call you? What is your will?   10
SHYLOCK
I am bid forth to supper, Jessica.
There are my keys. But wherefore should I go?   12
I am not bid for love, they flatter me;
But yet I'll go in hate to feed upon
The prodigal Christian. Jessica my girl,
Look to my house. I am right loath to go.

---

34 *gentle* (with pun on "gentile"?)   35 *never dare misfortune* may misfortune
never dare   36 *she* i.e., misfortune   37 *she* i.e., Jessica; *issue* offspring; *faithless* i.e., not Christian, but Lorenzo's actions are also *faithless*
   II.5 Shylock's house   2 *of* between   5 *rend apparel out* wear out clothing
through tearing   12 *wherefore* why

There is some ill a-brewing towards my rest,
18 For I did dream of money bags tonight.
LANCELOT   I beseech you, sir, go. My young master doth
20 expect your reproach.
SHYLOCK   So do I his.
LANCELOT   And they have conspired together. I will not
say you shall see a masque, but if you do, then it was
24 not for nothing that my nose fell a-bleeding on Black
25 Monday last at six o'clock i' th' morning, falling out
that year on Ash Wednesday was four year in th' afternoon.
SHYLOCK
What, are there masques? Hear you me, Jessica:
Lock up my doors; and when you hear the drum
30 And the vile squealing of the wry-necked fife,
Clamber not you up to the casements then,
Nor thrust your head into the public street
33 To gaze on Christian fools with varnished faces;
But stop my house's ears – I mean my casements;
35 Let not the sound of shallow foppery enter
36 My sober house. By Jacob's staff I swear
I have no mind of feasting forth tonight;
But I will go. Go you before me, sirrah.
Say I will come.
LANCELOT   I will go before, sir.
40 Mistress, look out at window for all this:
There will come a Christian by
42   Will be worth a Jewès eye.   *[Exit.]*

---

18 *money bags* (Elizabethan dream interpretation worked by contraries, so to
dream of money was a prediction of its loss); *tonight* last night   **20** *reproach*
i.e., "approach," but the error is also wordplay, as Shylock makes clear   **24–
25** *Black Monday* Easter Monday   **25–27** *falling . . . afternoon* (Lancelot departs into a gibberish of omens and fortune-telling)   **30** *wry-necked fife* i.e.,
played with a musician's head awry (?)   **33** *varnished faces* painted masks
35 *foppery* frivolity   **36** *By . . . staff* (an appropriate oath because Jacob set
out from his homeland with only a staff and returned twenty years later a
wealthy man: see Genesis 32:10)   **42** *Jewès eye* object of great value (the di-
syllabic form of "Jew-es" is needed for the meter)

SHYLOCK
  What says that fool of Hagar's offspring? Ha?   43
JESSICA
  His words were "Farewell, mistress," nothing else.
SHYLOCK
  The patch is kind enough, but a huge feeder,   45
  Snail-slow in profit, and he sleeps by day   46
  More than the wildcat. Drones hive not with me,
  Therefore I part with him, and part with him
  To one that I would have him help to waste
  His borrowed purse. Well, Jessica, go in.   50
  Perhaps I will return immediately.
  Do as I bid you; shut doors after you.
  Fast bind, fast find: 53
  A proverb never stale in thrifty mind.   *Exit.*
JESSICA
  Farewell; and if my fortune be not crost,
  I have a father, you a daughter, lost.   *Exit.*
                    *

❧ **II.6** *Enter the Masquers, Gratiano and Salarino.*

GRATIANO
  This is the penthouse under which Lorenzo   1
  Desired us to make stand.   2
SALARINO   His hour is almost past.
GRATIANO
  And it is marvel he outdwells his hour,
  For lovers ever run before the clock.
SALARINO
  O ten times faster Venus' pigeons fly   5
  To seal love's bonds new made than they are wont

---

43 *Hagar's offspring* i.e., a gentile and an outcast (Hagar, Abraham's Egyptian bondwoman, bore Ishmael, and both became gentile outcasts: see Genesis 16 and 21:9)   45 *patch* fool   46 *profit* productive work   53 *Fast* secure
  II.6 Shylock's house   1 *penthouse* projecting upper story of a building   2 *make stand* wait   5 *Venus' pigeons* doves that draw her chariot

7   To keep obligèd faith unforfeited!

GRATIANO

That ever holds. Who riseth from a feast
With that keen appetite that he sits down?
10   Where is the horse that doth untread again
His tedious measures with the unbated fire
That he did pace them first? All things that are
Are with more spirit chasèd than enjoyed.
14   How like a younger or a prodigal
15   The scarfèd bark puts from her native bay,
Hugged and embracèd by the strumpet wind!
How like the prodigal doth she return,
With overweathered ribs and ragged sails,
Lean, rent, and beggared by the strumpet wind!
          Enter Lorenzo.

SALARINO

20   Here comes Lorenzo; more of this hereafter.

LORENZO

21   Sweet friends, your patience for my long abode.
Not I but my affairs have made you wait.
23   When you shall please to play the thieves for wives,
24   I'll watch as long for you then. Approach;
25   Here dwells my father Jew. Ho! Who's within?
          [Enter] Jessica above [in a page's clothes].

JESSICA

Who are you? Tell me for more certainty,
Albeit I'll swear that I do know your tongue.

LORENZO

Lorenzo, and thy love.

JESSICA

Lorenzo certain, and my love indeed,
30   For who love I so much? And now who knows
But you, Lorenzo, whether I am yours?

---

7 *obligèd* bound by marriage or marriage contract; *unforfeited* unbroken
14–17 *How . . . return* (see Luke 15:11–32 for the parable of the Prodigal
Son, which is alluded to here) 14 *younger* i.e., younger son 15 *scarfèd*
decked with flags or streamers 21 *abode* delay 23 *play the thieves for* steal
24 *watch* wait 25 *father* i.e., father-in-law to be

LORENZO
　Heaven and thy thoughts are witness that thou art.
JESSICA
　Here, catch this casket; it is worth the pains.
　I am glad 'tis night, you do not look on me,
　For I am much ashamed of my exchange.   35
　But love is blind, and lovers cannot see
　The pretty follies that themselves commit;
　For if they could, Cupid himself would blush
　To see me thus transformèd to a boy.
LORENZO
　Descend, for you must be my torchbearer.   40
JESSICA
　What, must I hold a candle to my shames?
　They in themselves, good sooth, are too too light.   42
　Why, 'tis an office of discovery, love,   43
　And I should be obscured.
LORENZO   So are you, sweet,
　Even in the lovely garnish of a boy.   45
　But come at once,
　For the close night doth play the runaway,   47
　And we are stayed for at Bassanio's feast.   48
JESSICA
　I will make fast the doors, and gild myself   49
　With some more ducats, and be with you straight.   50
　　　　　　　　　　　　　　　　　　　[Exit above.]
GRATIANO
　Now by my hood, a gentle and no Jew!   51
LORENZO
　Beshrew me but I love her heartily!   52
　For she is wise, if I can judge of her,

---

35 *exchange* change of clothes (but also "theft" and "elopement") **42** *light*
frivolous, immodest (with pun on moral "lightness") **43** *'tis . . . discovery*
i.e., to bear a torch is to reveal **45** *garnish* dress, trimmings **47** *close* secret;
doth . . . runaway i.e., is passing rapidly **48** *stayed for* awaited **49** *gild* cover
in gold leaf (i.e., make more valuable, but also "brighten") **51** *by . . . hood*
(meaningless emphatic phrase); *gentle* gentile **52** *Beshrew me* evil come to
me (a weak oath)

And fair she is, if that mine eyes be true,
And true she is, as she hath proved herself;
And therefore, like herself, wise, fair, and true,
Shall she be placèd in my constant soul.
     Enter Jessica [below].
What, art thou come? On, gentlemen, away!
Our masquing mates by this time for us stay.
                              Exit [with Jessica and Salarino].

     Enter Antonio.
60 ANTONIO   Who's there?
    GRATIANO   Signor Antonio?
    ANTONIO
       Fie, fie, Gratiano! Where are all the rest?
       'Tis nine o'clock; our friends all stay for you.
       No masque tonight. The wind is come about;
65   Bassanio presently will go aboard.
       I have sent twenty out to seek for you.
    GRATIANO
       I am glad on't. I desire no more delight
       Than to be under sail and gone tonight.   *Exeunt.*
                              *

     ∾ **II.7** *[Flourish of cornets.] Enter Portia with Morocco
     and both their trains.*

    PORTIA
1   Go, draw aside the curtains and discover
2   The several caskets to this noble prince.
       Now make your choice.
    MOROCCO
       This first, of gold, who this inscription bears,
       "Who chooseth me shall gain what many men desire."
       The second, silver, which this promise carries,
       "Who chooseth me shall get as much as he deserves."

  ─────────
  65 *presently* immediately
  II.7 Portia's house, Belmont   1 *discover* reveal   2 *several* various

This third, dull lead, with warning all as blunt,   8
"Who chooseth me must give and hazard all he hath."
How shall I know if I do choose the right?   10
PORTIA
The one of them contains my picture, prince.
If you choose that, then I am yours withal.
MOROCCO
Some god direct my judgment! Let me see:
I will survey th' inscriptions back again.
What says this leaden casket?
"Who chooseth me must give and hazard all he hath."
Must give – for what? for lead! Hazard for lead?
This casket threatens; men that hazard all
Do it in hope of fair advantages.
A golden mind stoops not to shows of dross;   20
I'll then nor give nor hazard aught for lead.   21
What says the silver with her virgin hue?
"Who chooseth me shall get as much as he deserves."
As much as he deserves? Pause there, Morocco,
And weigh thy value with an even hand: 25
If thou be'st rated by thy estimation,   26
Thou dost deserve enough; and yet enough
May not extend so far as to the lady;
And yet to be afeard of my deserving
Were but a weak disabling of myself.   30
As much as I deserve? Why that's the lady.
I do in birth deserve her, and in fortunes,
In graces, and in qualities of breeding;
But more than these, in love I do deserve.
What if I strayed no farther, but chose here?
Let's see once more this saying graved in gold:
"Who chooseth me shall gain what many men desire."
Why that's the lady! All the world desires her;

---

8 *blunt* i.e., the casket is plain, *dull* as *lead*   21 *nor . . . nor* neither . . . nor
25 *with . . . hand* impartially   26 *estimation* reputation   30 *disabling* under-
rating

From the four corners of the earth they come
40   To kiss this shrine, this mortal breathing saint.
41   The Hyrcanian deserts and the vasty wilds
Of wide Arabia are as throughfares now
For princes to come view fair Portia.
44   The watery kingdom, whose ambitious head
Spits in the face of heaven, is no bar
46   To stop the foreign spirits, but they come
As o'er a brook to see fair Portia.
One of these three contains her heavenly picture.
Is't like that lead contains her? 'Twere damnation
50   To think so base a thought; it were too gross
51   To rib her cerecloth in the obscure grave.
Or shall I think in silver she's immured,
53   Being ten times undervalued to tried gold?
O sinful thought! Never so rich a gem
Was set in worse than gold. They have in England
56   A coin that bears the figure of an angel
57   Stamped in gold; but that's insculped upon:
But here an angel in a golden bed
Lies all within. Deliver me the key.
60   Here do I choose, and thrive I as I may!

PORTIA
    There, take it, prince; and if my form lie there,
    Then I am yours.
      [He opens the golden casket.]
MOROCCO   O hell! What have we here?
63   A carrion death, within whose empty eye
There is a written scroll! I'll read the writing.

---

40 *mortal breathing* living   **41** *Hyrcanian deserts* i.e., wilderness area south-east of the Caspian Sea, noted for fierce tigers since classical times   **44** *watery kingdom* i.e., Neptune's realm, the seas   **46** *foreign spirits* i.e., spirited (courageous) foreigners (Portia's other suitors)   **50** *it* i.e., lead   **51** *rib* cover, enclose; *cerecloth* waxed cloth used in wrapping for burial; *obscure* (accent on first syllable)   **53** *tried* tested, assayed   **56** *coin . . . angel* i.e., the "angel," a coin with a winged Saint Michael's image   **57** *insculped upon* engraved on the surface   **63** *death* death's-head, skull

"All that glisters is not gold;   65
Often have you heard that told.
Many a man his life hath sold
But my outside to behold.   68
Gilded tombs do worms infold.
Had you been as wise as bold,   70
Young in limbs, in judgment old,
Your answer had not been inscrolled.   72
Fare you well, your suit is cold."
Cold indeed, and labor lost.
Then farewell heat, and welcome frost!   75
Portia, adieu. I have too grieved a heart
To take a tedious leave. Thus losers part.
                    Exit [with his train. Flourish of cornets].

PORTIA
A gentle riddance. Draw the curtains, go.
Let all of his complexion choose me so.   *Exeunt.* 79
                        *

❧ **II.8** *Enter Salarino and Solanio.*

SALARINO
Why, man, I saw Bassanio under sail;
With him is Gratiano gone along,
And in their ship I am sure Lorenzo is not.
SOLANIO
The villain Jew with outcries raised the duke,   4
Who went with him to search Bassanio's ship.
SALARINO
He came too late – the ship was under sail,
But there the duke was given to understand

---

65 *glisters* glitters 68 *my outside* i.e., my shining surface 72 *inscrolled* thus inscribed 75 *heat* i.e., of love, now *labor lost* (l. 74) 79 *complexion* (1) skin's appearance (see II.1.1), (2) temperament, personality (hence, a person who would choose the gold casket)
II.8 A street in Venice 4 *raised* aroused

That in a gondola were seen together
Lorenzo and his amorous Jessica.
10   Besides, Antonio certified the duke
They were not with Bassanio in his ship.

SOLANIO
I never heard a passion so confused,
So strange, outrageous, and so variable
As the dog Jew did utter in the streets:
"My daughter! O my ducats! O my daughter!
Fled with a Christian! O my Christian ducats!
Justice! The law! My ducats and my daughter!
A sealèd bag, two sealèd bags of ducats,
Of double ducats, stolen from me by my daughter!
20   And jewels – two stones, two rich and precious stones,
Stolen by my daughter! Justice! Find the girl!
She hath the stones upon her, and the ducats!"

SALARINO
Why, all the boys in Venice follow him,
Crying his stones, his daughter, and his ducats.

SOLANIO
25   Let good Antonio look he keep his day,
Or he shall pay for this.

SALARINO   Marry, well remembered.
27   I reasoned with a Frenchman yesterday,
Who told me, in the narrow seas that part
The French and English there miscarrièd
30   A vessel of our country richly fraught.
I thought upon Antonio when he told me,
And wished in silence that it were not his.

SOLANIO
You were best to tell Antonio what you hear.
Yet do not suddenly, for it may grieve him.

---

10 *certified* authoritatively attested (to)   **20** *stones* jewels (but also slang for "testicles," a bawdy joke about emasculation – as the boys and their cries, ll. 23–24, make clear)   **25** *keep his day* repay his debt on the day agreed   **27** *reasoned* talked   **30** *fraught* loaded

SALARINO
A kinder gentleman treads not the earth.
I saw Bassanio and Antonio part:
Bassanio told him he would make some speed
Of his return; he answered, "Do not so.
Slubber not business for my sake, Bassanio,   39
But stay the very riping of the time;   40
And for the Jew's bond which he hath of me,
Let it not enter in your mind of love.   42
Be merry, and employ your chiefest thoughts
To courtship and such fair ostents of love   44
As shall conveniently become you there."
And even there, his eye being big with tears,
Turning his face, he put his hand behind him,
And with affection wondrous sensible   48
He wrung Bassanio's hand; and so they parted.

SOLANIO
I think he only loves the world for him.   50
I pray thee let us go and find him out
And quicken his embracèd heaviness   52
With some delight or other.

SALARINO   Do we so.   *Exeunt.*

                              *

∾ **II.9** *Enter Nerissa and a Servitor.*

NERISSA
Quick, quick, I pray thee, draw the curtain straight.   1
The Prince of Aragon hath ta'en his oath,
And comes to his election presently.   3
    *[Flourish of cornets.] Enter Aragon, his train, and
    Portia.*

---

39 *Slubber* perform hastily, botch   42 *mind of love* thoughts of wooing   44
ostents shows   48 *wondrous sensible* wonderfully strong in feeling   52
quicken . . . heaviness enliven the sadness he has embraced
  II.9 Portia's house, Belmont   1 *draw* pull; *curtain* i.e., the one hiding the
caskets; *straight* at once   3 *election* choice; *presently* immediately

PORTIA
    Behold, there stand the caskets, noble prince.
    If you choose that wherein I am contained,
    Straight shall our nuptial rites be solemnized;
    But if you fail, without more speech, my lord,
    You must be gone from hence immediately.

ARAGON
    I am enjoined by oath to observe three things:
10 First, never to unfold to any one
    Which casket 'twas I chose; next, if I fail
    Of the right casket, never in my life
    To woo a maid in way of marriage;
    Lastly, if I do fail in fortune of my choice,
    Immediately to leave you and be gone.

PORTIA
    To these injunctions every one doth swear
    That comes to hazard for my worthless self.

ARAGON
18 And so have I addressed me. Fortune now
    To my heart's hope! Gold, silver, and base lead.
20 "Who chooseth me must give and hazard all he hath."
21 You shall look fairer ere I give or hazard.
    What says the golden chest? Ha, let me see:
    "Who chooseth me shall gain what many men desire."
24 What many men desire – that "many" may be meant
    By the fool multitude that choose by show,
26 Not learning more than the fond eye doth teach,
27 Which pries not to th' interior, but like the martlet
28 Builds in the weather on the outward wall,
29 Even in the force and road of casualty.
30 I will not choose what many men desire,

-----

18 *addressed me* prepared myself (i.e., by thus swearing); *Fortune* good luck
21 *You . . . hazard* (addressed to the leaden casket) 24–25 *meant / By* intended to mean, to suggest 26 *fond* foolish 27 *martlet* a bird (Aragon may
make a mistaken analogy here, since the martlet was often used as an image
of prudence) 28 *in* exposed to 29 *force . . . casualty* power and path of
mishap

Because I will not jump with common spirits   31
And rank me with the barbarous multitudes.
Why then, to thee, thou silver treasure house:
Tell me once more what title thou dost bear.
"Who chooseth me shall get as much as he deserves."
And well said too, for who shall go about
To cozen fortune, and be honorable   37
Without the stamp of merit? Let none presume
To wear an undeservèd dignity.
O that estates, degrees, and offices   40
Were not derived corruptly, and that clear honor
Were purchased by the merit of the wearer!
How many then should cover that stand bare,   43
How many be commanded that command;
How much low peasantry would then be gleaned   45
From the true seed of honor, and how much honor   46
Picked from the chaff and ruin of the times
To be new varnished. Well, but to my choice.   48
"Who chooseth me shall get as much as he deserves."
I will assume desert. Give me a key for this,   50
And instantly unlock my fortunes here.
     [He opens the silver casket.]
PORTIA
Too long a pause for that which you find there.
ARAGON
What's here? The portrait of a blinking idiot
Presenting me a schedule! I will read it.   54
How much unlike art thou to Portia!
How much unlike my hopes and my deservings!
"Who chooseth me shall have as much as he deserves."
Did I deserve no more than a fool's head?
Is that my prize? Are my deserts no better?

---

31 *jump with* go along with   **37** *cozen* cheat   **40** *estates, degrees* social ranks
43 *cover . . . bare* wear hats who now stand bareheaded (i.e., retain the dignity of wearing their hats rather than removing them in deference)   **45**
gleaned culled   **46** *honor* noble rank   **48** *new varnished* refurbished   **54**
schedule scroll

PORTIA

60   To offend and judge are distinct offices,
      And of opposèd natures.

ARAGON   What is here?

62   "The fire seven times tried this;
           Seven times tried that judgment is
           That did never choose amiss.

65   Some there be that shadows kiss;
           Such have but a shadow's bliss.

67   There be fools alive iwis,
           Silvered o'er, and so was this.
           Take what wife you will to bed,

70   I will ever be your head.

71   So be gone, you are sped."
      Still more fool I shall appear
      By the time I linger here.
      With one fool's head I came to woo,
      But I go away with two.
      Sweet, adieu. I'll keep my oath,

77   Patiently to bear my wroath.   *[Exit with his train.]*

PORTIA
      Thus hath the candle singed the moth.

79   O these deliberate fools! When they do choose,

80   They have the wisdom by their wit to lose.

NERISSA
      The ancient saying is no heresy:
      Hanging and wiving goes by destiny.

PORTIA
      Come draw the curtain, Nerissa.
        Enter Messenger.

MESSENGER
      Where is my lady?

PORTIA   Here. What would my lord?

60–61 *To offend . . . natures* i.e., those who are subject to judgment may not be their own judges   **62** *this* i.e., the silver   **65** *shadows* illusive images   **67** *iwis* certainly   **71** *sped* done for   **77** *wroath* (the quarto's word could mean "wrath" or "ruth," grief)   **79** *deliberate* reasoning, deliberating

MESSENGER
   Madam, there is alighted at your gate
   A young Venetian, one that comes before
   To signify th' approaching of his lord,
   From whom he bringeth sensible regreets,   88
   To wit, besides commends and courteous breath,
   Gifts of rich value. Yet I have not seen   90
   So likely an ambassador of love.
   A day in April never came so sweet
   To show how costly summer was at hand,   93
   As this forespurrer comes before his lord.   94
PORTIA
   No more, I pray thee. I am half afeard
   Thou wilt say anon he is some kin to thee,
   Thou spend'st such high-day wit in praising him.   97
   Come, come, Nerissa, for I long to see
   Quick Cupid's post that comes so mannerly.   99
NERISSA
   Bassanio, Lord Love, if thy will it be!   *Exeunt.*   100

*

❧ III.1 *[Enter] Solanio and Salarino.*

SOLANIO   Now what news on the Rialto?
SALARINO   Why, yet it lives there unchecked that Anto-   2
nio hath a ship of rich lading wrecked on the narrow
seas – the Goodwins I think they call the place, a very   4
dangerous flat, and fatal, where the carcasses of many a

---

88 *sensible regreets* tangible greetings (i.e., more than words)   93 *costly* rich,
bountiful   94 *forespurrer* forerunner   97 *highday* holiday (i.e., suitable for a
special occasion)   99 *post* messenger   100 *Lord Love* god of love (i.e.,
Cupid)
   III.1 A street in Venice   2 *lives* i.e., circulates; *unchecked* uncontradicted
4 *Goodwins* Goodwin Sands (dangerous shoal off the southeastern English
coast)

6 tall ship lie buried as they say, if my gossip Report be an
   honest woman of her word.

SOLANIO   I would she were as lying a gossip in that as
9 ever knapped ginger or made her neighbors believe she
10 wept for the death of a third husband. But it is true,
11 without any slips of prolixity or crossing the plain high-
   way of talk, that the good Antonio, the honest Antonio – O that I had a title good enough to keep his
   name company! –

15 SALARINO   Come, the full stop!

SOLANIO   Ha, what sayest thou? Why the end is, he hath
   lost a ship.

SALARINO   I would it might prove the end of his losses.

19 SOLANIO   Let me say "amen" betimes lest the devil cross
20 my prayer, for here he comes in the likeness of a Jew.
        Enter Shylock.
   How now, Shylock? What news among the merchants?

SHYLOCK   You knew, none so well, none so well as you,
   of my daughter's flight.

SALARINO   That's certain. I for my part knew the tailor
25 that made the wings she flew withal.

SOLANIO   And Shylock for his own part knew the bird
27 was fledge, and then it is the complexion of them all to
28 leave the dam.

SHYLOCK   She is damned for it.

30 SALARINO   That's certain, if the devil may be her judge.

SHYLOCK   My own flesh and blood to rebel!

32 SOLANIO   Out upon it, old carrion! Rebels it at these
   years?

SHYLOCK   I say my daughter is my flesh and my blood.

---

6 *gossip Report* (a humorous comparison of *Report* – rumor – to a neighborly
or friendly source of information, a *gossip*)   9 *knapped* nibbled   11 *slips of
prolixity* lapses into wordiness   11–12 *crossing . . . talk* i.e., deviation from
plain speech   15 *full stop* period, end of statement (Salarino is tired of his
friend's verbosity)   19 *cross* thwart   25 *wings* i.e., the page's suit (with pun
on *flight*)   27 *fledge* ready to fly; *complexion* disposition   28 *dam* mother
(i.e., parent)   32 *carrion* dead, putrefied flesh (cf. II.7.63) 32–33 *Rebels . . .
years* i.e., do you have fleshly desires at your age

SALARINO   There is more difference between thy flesh
and hers than between jet and ivory, more between   36
your bloods than there is between red wine and Rhenish. But tell us, do you hear whether Antonio have had
any loss at sea or no?

SHYLOCK   There I have another bad match! A bankrupt,   40
a prodigal, who dare scarce show his head on the Rialto, a beggar that was used to come so smug upon the
mart! Let him look to his bond. He was wont to call me   43
usurer. Let him look to his bond. He was wont to lend
money for a Christian courtesy. Let him look to his
bond.

SALARINO   Why, I am sure if he forfeit thou wilt not take
his flesh. What's that good for?

SHYLOCK   To bait fish withal. If it will feed nothing else,
it will feed my revenge. He hath disgraced me and hin-   50
dered me half a million, laughed at my losses, mocked
at my gains, scorned my nation, thwarted my bargains,
cooled my friends, heated mine enemies – and what's
his reason? I am a Jew. Hath not a Jew eyes? Hath not a
Jew hands, organs, dimensions, senses, affections, pas-   55
sions? – fed with the same food, hurt with the same
weapons, subject to the same diseases, healed by the
same means, warmed and cooled by the same winter
and summer as a Christian is? If you prick us, do we
not bleed? If you tickle us, do we not laugh? If you poi-   60
son us, do we not die? And if you wrong us, shall we
not revenge? If we are like you in the rest, we will re-
semble you in that. If a Jew wrong a Christian, what is   63
his humility? Revenge. If a Christian wrong a Jew, what
should his sufferance be by Christian example? Why re-   65
venge! The villainy you teach me I will execute, and it
shall go hard but I will better the instruction.

Enter a Man from Antonio.

---

36 *jet* a black stone   40 *match* bargain   43 *mart* exchange   55 *dimensions*
parts of the body   63–64 *what is his humility* i.e., how does the Christian ex-
press *humility* (Shylock is deeply ironic)   65 *his* i.e., the Jew's

MAN   Gentlemen, my master Antonio is at his house and
   desires to speak with you both.
70 SALARINO   We have been up and down to seek him.
   Enter Tubal.
71 SOLANIO   Here comes another of the tribe. A third cannot be matched, unless the devil himself turn Jew.
                    Exeunt [Solanio, Salarino, and Man].
SHYLOCK   How now, Tubal! What news from Genoa?
   Hast thou found my daughter?
TUBAL   I often came where I did hear of her, but cannot
   find her.
SHYLOCK   Why there, there, there, there! A diamond
   gone cost me two thousand ducats in Frankfurt! The
79 curse never fell upon our nation till now; I never felt it
80 till now. Two thousand ducats in that, and other precious, precious jewels. I would my daughter were dead
   at my foot, and the jewels in her ear! Would she were
   hearsed at my foot, and the ducats in her coffin. No
   news of them, why so? And I know not what's spent in
   the search. Why thou loss upon loss! The thief gone
   with so much, and so much to find the thief, and no
   satisfaction, no revenge, nor no ill luck stirring but
   what lights o' my shoulders, no sighs but o' my breathing, no tears but o' my shedding.
90 TUBAL   Yes, other men have ill luck too. Antonio, as I
   heard in Genoa –
SHYLOCK   What, what, what? Ill luck, ill luck?
TUBAL   Hath an argosy cast away coming from Tripolis.
SHYLOCK   I thank God, I thank God! Is it true, is it true?
TUBAL   I spoke with some of the sailors that escaped the
   wreck.
SHYLOCK   I thank thee, good Tubal. Good news, good
   news! Ha, ha! Heard in Genoa?

71–72 *cannot be matched* cannot be found to match them   79 *curse* (probably the prophecy of Jerusalem's destruction; see Matthew 23:38)

TUBAL   Your daughter spent in Genoa, as I heard, one   *100*
night fourscore ducats.

SHYLOCK   Thou stick'st a dagger in me. I shall never see
my gold again. Fourscore ducats at a sitting, fourscore
ducats!

TUBAL   There came divers of Antonio's creditors in my   *104*
company to Venice that swear he cannot choose but
break.   *106*

SHYLOCK   I am very glad of it. I'll plague him; I'll torture
him. I am glad of it.

TUBAL   One of them showed me a ring that he had of
your daughter for a monkey.   *110*

SHYLOCK   Out upon her! Thou torturest me, Tubal. It
was my turquoise; I had it of Leah when I was a bache-   *112*
lor. I would not have given it for a wilderness of mon-
keys.

TUBAL   But Antonio is certainly undone.

SHYLOCK   Nay, that's true, that's very true. Go, Tubal, fee   *116*
me an officer; bespeak him a fortnight before. I will   *117*
have the heart of him if he forfeit, for were he out of
Venice I can make what merchandise I will. Go, Tubal,   *119*
and meet me at our synagogue, go, good Tubal, at our   *120*
synagogue, Tubal.   *Exeunt.*

*

ᵔ **III.2** *Enter Bassanio, Portia, Gratiano, [Nerissa,] and
all their trains.*

PORTIA
I pray you tarry; pause a day or two
Before you hazard, for in choosing wrong
I lose your company. Therefore forbear awhile.

---

104 *divers* several   **106** *break* go bankrupt   **112** *Leah* (Shylock's wife)   **116**
fee hire   **117** *officer* arresting officer; *bespeak* engage   **119** *make . . . will*
drive what bargains I wish
   III.2 Portia's house, Belmont

There's something tells me, but it is not love,
I would not lose you; and you know yourself

6 Hate counsels not in such a quality.
But lest you should not understand me well –
And yet a maiden hath no tongue but thought –
I would detain you here some month or two

10 Before you venture for me. I could teach you
11 How to choose right, but then I am forsworn.
So will I never be. So may you miss me.
But if you do, you'll make me wish a sin –
That I had been forsworn. Beshrew your eyes!

15 They have o'erlooked me and divided me;
One half of me is yours, the other half yours –
Mine own I would say; but if mine then yours,

18 And so all yours! O these naughty times
Puts bars between the owners and their rights!

20 And so, though yours, not yours. Prove it so,
Let fortune go to hell for it, not I.

22 I speak too long, but 'tis to peize the time,
23 To eke it and to draw it out in length,
To stay you from election.

BASSANIO   Let me choose,
25 For as I am, I live upon the rack.

PORTIA
Upon the rack, Bassanio? Then confess
What treason there is mingled with your love.

BASSANIO
None but that ugly treason of mistrust
Which makes me fear th' enjoying of my love.

30 There may as well be amity and life
'Tween snow and fire, as treason and my love.

PORTIA
Ay, but I fear you speak upon the rack,

---

6 *quality* way   11 *forsworn* false to my oath   15 *o'erlooked* bewitched   18 *naughty* evil   20 *Prove it so* if it prove so   22 *peize* retard (the image is from adding weights to a clock)   23 *eke* increase   25–27 *upon the rack . . . treason* (refers to confessions of treason obtained by torture on the rack)

Where men enforcèd do speak anything.
BASSANIO
Promise me life and I'll confess the truth.
PORTIA
Well then, confess and live.
BASSANIO   Confess and love
Had been the very sum of my confession!
O happy torment, when my torturer
Doth teach me answers for deliverance.
But let me to my fortune and the caskets.
PORTIA
Away then! I am locked in one of them;   40
If you do love me, you will find me out.
Nerissa and the rest, stand all aloof.
Let music sound while he doth make his choice;
Then if he lose he makes a swanlike end,   44
Fading in music. That the comparison
May stand more proper, my eye shall be the stream
And watery deathbed for him. He may win;
And what is music then? Then music is
Even as the flourish when true subjects bow   49
To a new-crownèd monarch. Such it is   50
As are those dulcet sounds in break of day
That creep into the dreaming bridegroom's ear
And summon him to marriage. Now he goes,
With no less presence but with much more love
Than young Alcides when he did redeem   55
The virgin tribute paid by howling Troy
To the sea monster. I stand for sacrifice.   57
The rest aloof are the Dardanian wives,   58
With blearèd visages come forth to view   59
The issue of th' exploit. Go, Hercules!   60

---

44 *swanlike end* (the ordinarily mute swan was thought to sing just before death) **49** *flourish* sounding of trumpets **55–57** *Alcides . . . monster* (Alcides, or Hercules, rescued the daughter of the Trojan king from sacrifice to a sea monster) **57** *stand for sacrifice* represent the sacrificial victim **58** *Dardanian* Trojan **59** *blearèd* tear-stained **60** *issue* outcome

61 Live thou, I live. With much, much more dismay
    I view the fight than thou that mak'st the fray.
        A song the whilst Bassanio comments on the caskets
        to himself.

63   Tell me where is fancy bred,
                Or in the heart, or in the head?
                How begot, how nourishèd?
                    Reply, reply.
                It is engendered in the eye,
                With gazing fed, and fancy dies
                In the cradle where it lies.
70   Let us all ring fancy's knell.
                    I'll begin it – Ding, dong, bell.
    ALL   Ding, dong, bell.

BASSANIO
73 So may the outward shows be least themselves;
    The world is still deceived with ornament.
    In law, what plea so tainted and corrupt
    But being seasoned with a gracious voice,
    Obscures the show of evil? In religion,
    What damnèd error but some sober brow
    Will bless it and approve it with a text,
80 Hiding the grossness with fair ornament?
81 There is no vice so simple but assumes
    Some mark of virtue on his outward parts.
    How many cowards whose hearts are all as false
    As stairs of sand, wear yet upon their chins
    The beards of Hercules and frowning Mars,
86 Who inward searched, have livers white as milk!
87 And these assume but valor's excrement
88 To render them redoubted. Look on beauty,

---

61 *Live thou* if you live   63 *fancy* fond love, infatuation   73 *be least them-*
selves i.e., belie the inner quality   81 *simple* unadulterated (but also implying
"simpleminded," "foolish")   86 *livers . . . milk* (cowards were supposed to
have white livers)   87 *excrement* outer growth (as hair)   88 *redoubted* feared

And you shall see 'tis purchased by the weight,   89
Which therein works a miracle in nature,   90
Making them lightest that wear most of it.   91
So are those crispèd snaky golden locks,   92
Which maketh such wanton gambols with the wind
Upon supposèd fairness, often known   94
To be the dowry of a second head,   95
The skull that bred them in the sepulcher.
Thus ornament is but the guilèd shore   97
To a most dangerous sea, the beauteous scarf
Veiling an Indian beauty; in a word,   99
The seeming truth which cunning times put on   100
To entrap the wisest. Therefore then, thou gaudy gold,
Hard food for Midas, I will none of thee;   102
Nor none of thee, thou pale and common drudge   103
'Tween man and man. But thou, thou meager lead
Which rather threaten'st than dost promise aught,
Thy paleness moves me more than eloquence;
And here choose I. Joy be the consequence!
PORTIA   [Aside]
How all the other passions fleet to air:
As doubtful thoughts, and rash-embraced despair,   109
And shudd'ring fear, and green-eyed jealousy.   110
O love, be moderate, allay thy ecstasy,
In measure rain thy joy, scant this excess!   112
I feel too much thy blessing. Make it less
For fear I surfeit.
BASSANIO   [Opening the leaden casket]
           What find I here?

---

89 *weight* (e.g., of cosmetics) 91 *lightest* least heavy (with pun on "light" in the sense of "light woman") 92 *crispèd* curled 94 *Upon supposèd fairness* on the head of a supposed beauty 95–96 *dowry . . . sepulcher* i.e., hair taken from a person now dead and buried 97 *guilèd* beguiling 99 *Indian* i.e., dark-skinned, not fair 102 *Midas* (all that Midas touched, including food, turned to gold) 103 *common drudge* everyone's servant (i.e., silver) 109 *As* such as 112 *scant* lessen

115   Fair Portia's counterfeit! What demigod
      Hath come so near creation? Move these eyes?
117   Or whether, riding on the balls of mine,
      Seem they in motion? Here are severed lips
      Parted with sugar breath; so sweet a bar
120   Should sunder such sweet friends. Here in her hairs
      The painter plays the spider, and hath woven
      A golden mesh t' entrap the hearts of men
123   Faster than gnats in cobwebs. But her eyes –
      How could he see to do them? Having made one,
      Methinks it should have power to steal both his
126   And leave itself unfurnished. Yet look, how far
127   The substance of my praise doth wrong this shadow
      In underprizing it, so far this shadow
129   Doth limp behind the substance. Here's the scroll,
130   The continent and summary of my fortune.
      [He reads.]
         "You that choose not by the view
132   Chance as fair, and choose as true.
         Since this fortune falls to you,
         Be content and seek no new.
         If you be well pleased with this
         And hold your fortune for your bliss,
         Turn you where your lady is,
138   And claim her with a loving kiss."
      A gentle scroll. Fair lady, by your leave,
140   I come by note, to give and to receive.
      Like one of two contending in a prize
      That thinks he hath done well in people's eyes,

---

115 *counterfeit* image, portrait   115–16 *What demigod . . . creation* i.e., only a demigod could have painted such a lifelike picture   117 *Or whether* or   120 *sweet friends* i.e., the two lips   123 *Faster* more securely   126 *unfurnished* without a companion eye   127 *shadow* picture   129 *substance* i.e., the real Portia   130 *continent* container   132 *Chance as fair* hazard as fortunately   138 *kiss* (the quarto does not specify when or how often Portia and Bassanio kiss)   140 *come by note* come according to the scroll

Hearing applause and universal shout,
Giddy in spirit, still gazing in a doubt
Whether those peals of praise be his or no –   145
So, thrice-fair lady, stand I even so,
As doubtful whether what I see be true,
Until confirmed, signed, ratified by you.

PORTIA
You see me, Lord Bassanio, where I stand,
Such as I am. Though for myself alone   *150*
I would not be ambitious in my wish
To wish myself much better, yet for you
I would be trebled twenty times myself,
A thousand times more fair, ten thousand times
More rich, that only to stand high in your account,   155
I might in virtues, beauties, livings, friends,   156
Exceed account. But the full sum of me
Is sum of something – which to term in gross   158
Is an unlessoned girl, unschooled, unpracticed;
Happy in this, she is not yet so old   *160*
But she may learn; happier than this,
She is not bred so dull but she can learn;
Happiest of all, is that her gentle spirit
Commits itself to yours to be directed,
As from her lord, her governor, her king.   165
Myself and what is mine to you and yours
Is now converted. But now I was the lord   167
Of this fair mansion, master of my servants,
Queen o'er myself; and even now, but now,
This house, these servants, and this same myself   *170*
Are yours, my lord's. I give them with this ring,
Which when you part from, lose, or give away,
Let it presage the ruin of your love

---

145 *his* addressed to him   **155** *that* so that; *account* estimation   **156** *livings*
possessions   **158** *something* i.e., at least something; *term in gross* state in full
165 *from* by   **167** *converted* transferred; *But now* a moment ago

174 And be my vantage to exclaim on you.

BASSANIO
Madam, you have bereft me of all words.
Only my blood speaks to you in my veins,
177 And there is such confusion in my powers
As, after some oration fairly spoke
By a belovèd prince, there doth appear
180 Among the buzzing pleasèd multitude,
181 Where every something being blent together
Turns to a wild of nothing, save of joy
Expressed and not expressed. But when this ring
Parts from this finger, then parts life from hence;
O then be bold to say Bassanio's dead!

NERISSA
My lord and lady, it is now our time,
187 That have stood by and seen our wishes prosper,
To cry "good joy." Good joy, my lord and lady!

GRATIANO
My Lord Bassanio, and my gentle lady,
190 I wish you all the joy that you can wish –
For I am sure you can wish none from me;
And when your honors mean to solemnize
The bargain of your faith, I do beseech you
Even at that time I may be married too.

BASSANIO
195 With all my heart, so thou canst get a wife.

GRATIANO
I thank your lordship, you have got me one.
My eyes, my lord, can look as swift as yours:
You saw the mistress, I beheld the maid.
199 You loved, I loved; for intermission
200 No more pertains to me, my lord, than you.
Your fortune stood upon the caskets there,

---

174 *vantage . . . you* opportunity to denounce you 177 *powers* faculties
181 *something* i.e., individual remark or comment 187 *That* who 195 *so* if
199 *intermission* pausing

And so did mine too as the matter falls.
For wooing here until I sweat again,   203
And swearing till my very roof was dry   204
With oaths of love, at last – if promise last –   205
I got a promise of this fair one here
To have her love, provided that your fortune
Achieved her mistress.

PORTIA   Is this true, Nerissa?

NERISSA
Madam, it is, so you stand pleased withal.   209

BASSANIO
And do you, Gratiano, mean good faith?   210

GRATIANO   Yes, faith, my lord.

BASSANIO
Our feast shall be much honored in your marriage.

GRATIANO   We'll play with them the first boy for a thou- 213
sand ducats.

NERISSA   What, and stake down?   215

GRATIANO   No, we shall ne'er win at that sport, and stake 216
down.
But who comes here? Lorenzo and his infidel!   218
What, and my old Venetian friend Salerio!
     Enter Lorenzo, Jessica, and Salerio, a messenger from
     Venice.

BASSANIO
Lorenzo and Salerio, welcome hither,   220
If that the youth of my new interest here   221
Have power to bid you welcome. By your leave,
I bid my very friends and countrymen,
Sweet Portia, welcome.

PORTIA   So do I, my lord.

---

203 *again* repeatedly   **204** *roof* (of the mouth)   **205** *if promise last* i.e., if
Nerissa's promise is still good   **209** *so . . . withal* if it pleases you   **213–14**
play . . . ducats wager a thousand ducats, the couple having the first boy to be
the winner   **215** *stake down* bets made with cash down   **216–17** *stake down*
(Gratiano quibbles on the meaning "limp penis")   **218** *infidel* i.e., Jessica
221 *interest* position in the household

They are entirely welcome.

LORENZO
I thank your honor. For my part, my lord,
My purpose was not to have seen you here,
But meeting with Salerio by the way,
He did entreat me past all saying nay
230 To come with him along.

SALERIO   I did, my lord,
And I have reason for it. Signor Antonio
232 Commends him to you.
        [Gives Bassanio a letter.]

BASSANIO   Ere I ope his letter,
I pray you tell me how my good friend doth.

SALERIO
Not sick, my lord, unless it be in mind,
Nor well unless in mind. His letters there
236 Will show you his estate.
        Open the letter.

GRATIANO
Nerissa, cheer yond stranger, bid her welcome.
Your hand, Salerio. What's the news from Venice?
239 How doth that royal merchant, good Antonio?
240 I know he will be glad of our success;
241 We are the Jasons, we have won the fleece.

SALERIO
I would you had won the fleece that he hath lost!

PORTIA
243 There are some shrewd contents in yond same paper
That steals the color from Bassanio's cheek:
Some dear friend dead, else nothing in the world
Could turn so much the constitution
Of any constant man. What, worse and worse?
With leave, Bassanio, I am half yourself,
And I must freely have the half of anything

---

232 *Commends him* sends his greetings 236 *estate* condition 239 *royal merchant* i.e., a "king" among merchants 241 *Jasons . . . fleece* (see I.1.170–72) 243 *shrewd* cursed, bitter

That this same paper brings you.   *250*

BASSANIO   O sweet Portia,
Here are a few of the unpleasant'st words
That ever blotted paper. Gentle lady,
When I did first impart my love to you,
I freely told you all the wealth I had
Ran in my veins – I was a gentleman –
And then I told you true; and yet, dear lady,
Rating myself at nothing, you shall see
How much I was a braggart. When I told you
My state was nothing, I should then have told you   *259*
That I was worse than nothing; for indeed   *260*
I have engaged myself to a dear friend,   *261*
Engaged my friend to his mere enemy   *262*
To feed my means. Here is a letter, lady,
The paper as the body of my friend,
And every word in it a gaping wound
Issuing lifeblood. But is it true, Salerio?
Hath all his ventures failed? What, not one hit?
From Tripolis, from Mexico, and England,
From Lisbon, Barbary, and India,
And not one vessel scape the dreadful touch   *270*
Of merchant-marring rocks?   *271*

SALERIO   Not one, my lord.
Besides, it should appear that if he had
The present money to discharge the Jew,   *273*
He would not take it. Never did I know   *274*
A creature that did bear the shape of man
So keen and greedy to confound a man.   *276*
He plies the duke at morning and at night,
And doth impeach the freedom of the state   *278*
If they deny him justice. Twenty merchants,
The duke himself, and the magnificoes   *280*

---

259 *state* estate, property **261** *engaged myself* become indebted **262** *mere* unqualified, sheer **271** *merchant* merchant ship **273** *discharge* pay off **274** *He* i.e., the Jew **276** *confound* ruin **278** *freedom . . . state* freedom of commerce, of contract, in Venice **280** *magnificoes* Venetian magnates

281   Of greatest port have all persuaded with him,
282   But none can drive him from the envious plea
      Of forfeiture, of justice, and his bond.

JESSICA
      When I was with him, I have heard him swear
      To Tubal and to Chus, his countrymen,
      That he would rather have Antonio's flesh
      Than twenty times the value of the sum
      That he did owe him; and I know, my lord,
      If law, authority, and power deny not,
290   It will go hard with poor Antonio.

PORTIA
      Is it your dear friend that is thus in trouble?

BASSANIO
      The dearest friend to me, the kindest man,
293   The best-conditioned and unwearied spirit
      In doing courtesies, and one in whom
      The ancient Roman honor more appears
      Than any that draws breath in Italy.

PORTIA
      What sum owes he the Jew?

BASSANIO
      For me, three thousand ducats.

PORTIA   What, no more?
299   Pay him six thousand, and deface the bond.
300   Double six thousand and then treble that,
      Before a friend of this description
      Shall lose a hair through Bassanio's fault.
      First go with me to church and call me wife,
      And then away to Venice to your friend!
      For never shall you lie by Portia's side
      With an unquiet soul. You shall have gold
      To pay the petty debt twenty times over;
      When it is paid, bring your true friend along.
      My maid Nerissa and myself meantime

---

281 *port* eminence; *persuaded* argued 282 *envious* malicious 293 *best-conditioned* best-natured 299 *deface* cancel

Will live as maids and widows. Come away,   *310*
For you shall hence upon your wedding day.   *311*
Bid your friends welcome, show a merry cheer;   *312*
Since you are dear bought, I will love you dear.
But let me hear the letter of your friend.
[BASSANIO *Reads.*] "Sweet Bassanio, my ships have all
   miscarried, my creditors grow cruel, my estate is very
   low, my bond to the Jew is forfeit. And since in paying
   it, it is impossible I should live, all debts are cleared be-
   tween you and I if I might but see you at my death.
   Notwithstanding, use your pleasure. If your love do not   *320*
   persuade you to come, let not my letter."

PORTIA
   O love! Dispatch all business and be gone.

BASSANIO
   Since I have your good leave to go away,
   I will make haste, but till I come again
   No bed shall e'er be guilty of my stay,
   Nor rest be interposer 'twixt us twain.   *Exeunt.*

                        *

❧ **III.3** *Enter [Shylock] the Jew and [Solanio and]*
       Antonio and the Jailer.

SHYLOCK
   Jailer, look to him. Tell not me of mercy.
   This is the fool that lent out money gratis.
   Jailer, look to him.

ANTONIO   Hear me yet, good Shylock.

SHYLOCK
   I'll have my bond, speak not against my bond,
   I have sworn an oath that I will have my bond.
   Thou call'dst me dog before thou hadst a cause,
   But since I am a dog, beware my fangs.   7

---

311 *hence* go hence   312 *cheer* countenance
   III.3 A street in Venice   7 *since . . . dog* i.e., now that I am acting like an
animal (some actors take this line literally and bark and snarl here)

The duke shall grant me justice. I do wonder,
9   Thou naughty jailer, that thou art so fond
10   To come abroad with him at his request.

ANTONIO
I pray thee hear me speak.

SHYLOCK
I'll have my bond. I will not hear thee speak,
I'll have my bond, and therefore speak no more.
14   I'll not be made a soft and dull-eyed fool,
To shake the head, relent, and sigh, and yield
To Christian intercessors. Follow not.
I'll have no speaking; I will have my bond.   *Exit.*

SOLANIO
It is the most impenetrable cur
19   That ever kept with men.

ANTONIO   Let him alone;
20   I'll follow him no more with bootless prayers.
He seeks my life. His reason well I know:
22   I oft delivered from his forfeitures
Many that have at times made moan to me.
Therefore he hates me.

SOLANIO   I am sure the duke
Will never grant this forfeiture to hold.

ANTONIO
The duke cannot deny the course of law;
27   For the commodity that strangers have
With us in Venice, if it be denied,
Will much impeach the justice of the state,
30   Since that the trade and profit of the city
Consisteth of all nations. Therefore go.
32   These griefs and losses have so bated me
That I shall hardly spare a pound of flesh
Tomorrow to my bloody creditor.

---

9 *naughty* wicked, corrupt; *fond* foolish   14 *dull-eyed* easily deceived   19
kept dwelled, associated   20 *bootless* fruitless   22 *delivered* saved   27 *commodity* benefit (i.e., trading rights or privileges); *strangers* non-Venetians, including Jews   32 *bated* reduced

Well, jailer, on. Pray God Bassanio come
To see me pay his debt, and then I care not!   *Exeunt.*

                              *

∾ III.4 *Enter Portia, Nerissa, Lorenzo, Jessica, and*
       [Balthasar,] a man of Portia's.

LORENZO
    Madam, although I speak it in your presence,
    You have a noble and a true conceit   2
    Of godlike amity, which appears most strongly   3
    In bearing thus the absence of your lord.
    But if you knew to whom you show this honor,
    How true a gentleman you send relief,
    How dear a lover of my lord your husband,
    I know you would be prouder of the work
    Than customary bounty can enforce you.   9
PORTIA
    I never did repent for doing good,   10
    Nor shall not now; for in companions
    That do converse and waste the time together,   12
    Whose souls do bear an equal yoke of love,
    There must be needs a like proportion
    Of lineaments, of manners, and of spirit;
    Which makes me think that this Antonio,
    Being the bosom lover of my lord,
    Must needs be like my lord. If it be so,
    How little is the cost I have bestowed
    In purchasing the semblance of my soul   20
    From out the state of hellish cruelty.
    This comes too near the praising of myself;
    Therefore no more of it. Hear other things:
    Lorenzo, I commit into your hands

III.4 Portia's house, Belmont **2** *conceit* conception, understanding **3**
amity friendship (i.e., that of Antonio and Bassanio) **9** *Than . . . you* than
ordinary kindness can make you **12** *waste* spend **20** *purchasing . . . soul*
i.e., redeeming Antonio, the likeness of Bassanio, *my soul*

25   The husbandry and manage of my house
        Until my lord's return. For mine own part,
        I have toward heaven breathed a secret vow
        To live in prayer and contemplation,
        Only attended by Nerissa here,
30   Until her husband and my lord's return.
        There is a monastery two miles off,
        And there we will abide. I do desire you
33   Not to deny this imposition,
        The which my love and some necessity
        Now lays upon you.

LORENZO   Madam, with all my heart;
        I shall obey you in all fair commands.

PORTIA
        My people do already know my mind
38   And will acknowledge you and Jessica
        In place of Lord Bassanio and myself.
40   So fare you well till we shall meet again.

LORENZO
        Fair thoughts and happy hours attend on you!

JESSICA
        I wish your ladyship all heart's content.

PORTIA
        I thank you for your wish, and am well pleased
        To wish it back on you. Fare you well, Jessica.
                        Exeunt [Jessica and Lorenzo].

        Now, Balthasar,
        As I have ever found thee honest-true,
        So let me find thee still. Take this same letter,
        And use thou all th' endeavor of a man
        In speed to Padua. See thou render this
50   Into my cousin's hands, Doctor Bellario;
51   And look, what notes and garments he doth give thee.
52   Bring them, I pray thee, with imagined speed

---

25 *husbandry* care 33 *imposition* duty, charge 38 *acknowledge* obey 51
look (an injunction: "pay attention to") 52 *imagined speed* swiftness of
thought (?), all imaginable speed (?)

Unto the traject, to the common ferry   53
Which trades to Venice. Waste no time in words
But get thee gone. I shall be there before thee.

BALTHASAR

Madam, I go with all convenient speed.   *[Exit.]* 56

PORTIA

Come on, Nerissa; I have work in hand
That you yet know not of. We'll see our husbands
Before they think of us.

NERISSA   Shall they see us?

PORTIA

They shall, Nerissa, but in such a habit   60
That they shall think we are accomplishèd   61
With that we lack. I'll hold thee any wager,   62
When we are both accoutered like young men,   63
I'll prove the prettier fellow of the two,
And wear my dagger with the braver grace,
And speak between the change of man and boy   66
With a reed voice, and turn two mincing steps   67
Into a manly stride, and speak of frays
Like a fine bragging youth, and tell quaint lies,   69
How honorable ladies sought my love,   70
Which I denying, they fell sick and died –
I could not do withal. Then I'll repent,   72
And wish, for all that, that I had not killed them.
And twenty of these puny lies I'll tell,
That men shall swear I have discontinued school
Above a twelvemonth. I have within my mind   76
A thousand raw tricks of these bragging jacks,   77
Which I will practice.   78

NERISSA   Why, shall we turn to men?

---

53 *traject* (from Italian *traghetto,* a ferry) **56** *convenient* appropriate **60** *habit* costume **61** *accomplishèd* equipped, completed **62** *that we lack* i.e., male genitals **63** *accoutered* dressed **66** *change . . . boy* i.e., puberty (when the voice breaks) **67** *reed* reedy, piping **69** *quaint* clever, contrived **72** *I . . . withal* I could not help it **76** *Above* more than (i.e., at least) **77** *raw* immature; *jacks* knaves **78** *turn to* turn into (with bawdy pun; cf. I.3.78)

PORTIA
   Fie, what a question's that,
80   If thou wert near a lewd interpreter!
   But come, I'll tell thee all my whole device
   When I am in my coach, which stays for us
   At the park gate; and therefore haste away,
   For we must measure twenty miles today.   *Exeunt.*

*

  III.5   *Enter [Lancelot the] Clown and Jessica.*

LANCELOT   Yes truly; for look you, the sins of the father
are to be laid upon the children. Therefore, I promise
3   you I fear you. I was always plain with you, and so now
4   I speak my agitation of the matter. Therefore be o' good
cheer, for truly I think you are damned. There is but
one hope in it that can do you any good, and that is but
7   a kind of bastard hope neither.
JESSICA   And what hope is that, I pray thee?
LANCELOT   Marry, you may partly hope that your father
10   got you not – that you are not the Jew's daughter.
JESSICA   That were a kind of bastard hope indeed! So the
sins of my mother should be visited upon me.
LANCELOT   Truly then, I fear you are damned both by father and mother. Thus when I shun Scylla your father,
15   I fall into Charybdis your mother. Well, you are gone
both ways.
JESSICA   I shall be saved by my husband. He hath made
me a Christian.
LANCELOT   Truly, the more to blame he! We were Chris-
20   tians enow before, e'en as many as could well live one
by another. This making of Christians will raise the

III.5 Portia's house   3 *fear you* am afraid for you; *plain* frank   4 *agitation*
(playing on "cogitation")   7 *neither* (simply emphasizes the statement)   15
fall into (with bawdy wordplay, "enter sexually"); *gone* done for   20 *enow be-*
fore i.e., numerous enough before Jessica became a Christian

price of hogs; if we grow all to be pork eaters, we shall
not shortly have a rasher on the coals for money.   23
    Enter Lorenzo.

JESSICA   I'll tell my husband, Lancelot, what you say.
Here he comes.

LORENZO   I shall grow jealous of you shortly, Lancelot, if
you thus get my wife into corners.

JESSICA   Nay, you need not fear us, Lorenzo. Lancelot and
I are out. He tells me flatly there's no mercy for me in   29
heaven because I am a Jew's daughter; and he says you   30
are no good member of the commonwealth, for in converting Jews to Christians you raise the price of pork.

LORENZO   *[To Lancelot]* I shall answer that better to the   33
commonwealth than you can the getting up of the
Negro's belly. The Moor is with child by you, Lancelot.   35

LANCELOT   It is much that the Moor should be more   36
than reason; but if she be less than an honest woman,   37
she is indeed more than I took her for.

LORENZO   How every fool can play upon the word! I
think the best grace of wit will shortly turn into silence,   40
and discourse grow commendable in none only but
parrots. Go in, sirrah; bid them prepare for dinner.

LANCELOT   That is done, sir. They have all stomachs.   43

LORENZO   Goodly Lord, what a wit-snapper are you!
Then bid them prepare dinner.

LANCELOT   That is done too, sir. Only "cover" is the word.   46

LORENZO   Will you cover then, sir?

LANCELOT   Not so, sir, neither! I know my duty.   48

LORENZO   Yet more quarreling with occasion! Wilt thou   49
show the whole wealth of thy wit in an instant? I pray   50
thee understand a plain man in his plain meaning: go

---

23 *rasher* thin slice (of bacon)   **29** *are out* have quarreled   **33** *answer* justify
35 *Moor* (the play's only mention of this character)   **36–37** *more than reason*
larger than is reasonable (with pun on *Moor*)   **37** *honest* chaste   **40** *best
grace* highest quality   **43** *stomachs* appetites   **46** *cover* i.e., lay the table   **48**
Not so . . . duty (to Lancelot *cover* now means to put on his cap; cf. II.9.43)
49 *quarreling with occasion* i.e., quibbling

to thy fellows, bid them cover the table, serve in the
meat, and we will come in to dinner.

54 LANCELOT   For the table, sir, it shall be served in; for the
55 meat, sir, it shall be covered; for your coming in to din-
56 ner, sir, why let it be as humors and conceits shall gov-
ern.   *Exit Clown [Lancelot].*

LORENZO
58 O dear discretion, how his words are suited!
The fool hath planted in his memory
60 An army of good words; and I do know
61 A many fools that stand in better place,
62 Garnished like him, that for a tricksy word
63 Defy the matter. How cheer'st thou, Jessica?
And now, good sweet, say thy opinion.
How dost thou like the Lord Bassanio's wife?

JESSICA
Past all expressing. It is very meet
The Lord Bassanio live an upright life
For having such a blessing in his lady;
He finds the joys of heaven here on earth,
70 And if on earth he do not merit it,
In reason he should never come to heaven.
Why, if two gods should play some heavenly match
73 And on the wager lay two earthly women,
74 And Portia one, there must be something else
75 Pawned with the other, for the poor rude world
Hath not her fellow.

LORENZO   Even such a husband
Hast thou of me as she is for a wife.

JESSICA
Nay, but ask my opinion too of that.

---

54 *table* (Lancelot quibbles with the word so that it now means the food itself)   55 *covered* served in a covered dish   56 *humors and conceits* whims
and ideas   58 *dear discretion* precious (or precise) discrimination; *suited* used
to suit the occasion   61 *A many* many; *stand . . . place* have higher social
rank   62 *Garnished like him* i.e., resembling him   63 *Defy the matter* i.e.,
refuse to talk sense; *How cheer'st thou* what cheer   73 *lay* bet   74 *else* more
75 *Pawned* staked

LORENZO
  I will anon. First let us go to dinner.
JESSICA
  Nay, let me praise you while I have a stomach.   80
LORENZO
  No, pray thee, let it serve for table talk;
  Then howsome'er thou speak'st, 'mong other things   82
  I shall digest it.   83
JESSICA   Well, I'll set you forth.
                                      Exit [with Lorenzo].

                            *

∾ **IV.1** *Enter the Duke, the Magnificoes, Antonio,*
    Bassanio, [Salerio,] and Gratiano [with others].

DUKE   What, is Antonio here?
ANTONIO   Ready, so please your grace.
DUKE
  I am sorry for thee. Thou art come to answer
  A stony adversary, an inhuman wretch,
  Uncapable of pity, void and empty   5
  From any dram of mercy.   6
ANTONIO   I have heard
  Your grace hath ta'en great pains to qualify   7
  His rigorous course; but since he stands obdurate,
  And that no lawful means can carry me
  Out of his envy's reach, I do oppose   10
  My patience to his fury, and am armed   11
  To suffer with a quietness of spirit
  The very tyranny and rage of his.
DUKE
  Go one, and call the Jew into the court.

---

80 *stomach* inclination, appetite   82 *howsome'er* however   83 *set you forth*
serve you up, as at a feast (i.e., praise you ironically)
    IV.1 A room in the doge's palace (often imagined as a court of justice)   5
Uncapable of without the capacity for   6 *From* of   7 *qualify* moderate, temper   10 *envy* malice   11 *armed* prepared

SALERIO

   He is ready at the door; he comes, my lord.
     Enter Shylock.

DUKE

16   Make room, and let him stand before our face.
   Shylock, the world thinks, and I think so too,
18   That thou but leadest this fashion of thy malice
19   To the last hour of act; and then 'tis thought
20   Thou'lt show thy mercy and remorse more strange
   Than is thy strange apparent cruelty;
   And where thou now exacts the penalty,
   Which is a pound of this poor merchant's flesh,
24   Thou wilt not only loose the forfeiture,
   But touched with human gentleness and love,
26   Forgive a moiety of the principal,
   Glancing an eye of pity on his losses,
   That have of late so huddled on his back,
29   Enow to press a royal merchant down
30   And pluck commiseration of his state
   From brassy bosoms and rough hearts of flint,
   From stubborn Turks and Tartars never trained
33   To offices of tender courtesy.
   We all expect a gentle answer, Jew.

SHYLOCK

35   I have possessed your grace of what I purpose,
36   And by our holy Sabaoth have I sworn
   To have the due and forfeit of my bond.
   If you deny it, let the danger light
39   Upon your charter and your city's freedom!
40   You'll ask me why I rather choose to have
   A weight of carrion flesh than to receive

---

16 *our* my (the "royal" plural) 18 *fashion* pretense 19 *last . . . act* very edge
of doing 20 *remorse* pity 20–21 *strange . . . strange* remarkable, unusual . . . extraordinary (or "alien"?) 24 *loose* let go 26 *moiety* portion 29
Enow enough; *royal merchant* (see III.2.239) 33 *offices* duties 35 *possessed*
informed 36 *Sabaoth* armies, hosts (Hebrew; Q2 and F read "Sabbath")
39 *freedom* (see III.2.278)

Three thousand ducats. I'll not answer that,
But say it is my humor. Is it answered?
What if my house be troubled with a rat,
And I be pleased to give ten thousand ducats
To have it baned? What, are you answered yet?   46
Some men there are love not a gaping pig,   47
Some that are mad if they behold a cat,
And others, when the bagpipe sings i' th' nose,
Cannot contain their urine; for affection,   50
Master of passion, sways it to the mood
Of what it likes or loathes. Now for your answer:
As there is no firm reason to be rendered
Why he cannot abide a gaping pig,   54
Why he a harmless necessary cat,
Why he a woolen bagpipe, but of force   56
Must yield to such inevitable shame
As to offend, himself being offended;
So can I give no reason, nor I will not,
More than a lodged hate and a certain loathing   60
I bear Antonio, that I follow thus
A losing suit against him. Are you answered?   62

BASSANIO
This is no answer, thou unfeeling man,
To excuse the current of thy cruelty!

SHYLOCK
I am not bound to please thee with my answers.

BASSANIO
Do all men kill the things they do not love?

SHYLOCK
Hates any man the thing he would not kill?

BASSANIO
Every offense is not a hate at first.   68

---

46 *baned* poisoned 47 *gaping pig* i.e., served roasted with its mouth
propped open 50 *affection* feeling, impulse 54–56 *he . . . he . . . he* i.e.,
one man . . . another . . . a third 56 *woolen bagpipe* i.e., with flannel-
covered bag; *of force* perforce, of necessity 60 *lodged* deep-seated 62 *losing*
unprofitable 68 *offense* injury, grievance

SHYLOCK
What, wouldst thou have a serpent sting thee twice?

ANTONIO
70 I pray you think you question with the Jew.
You may as well go stand upon the beach
72 And bid the main flood bate his usual height;
You may as well use question with the wolf
Why he hath made the ewe bleat for the lamb;
You may as well forbid the mountain pines
76 To wag their high tops and to make no noise
77 When they are fretten with the gusts of heaven;
You may as well do anything most hard
As seek to soften that – than which what's harder? –
80 His Jewish heart. Therefore I do beseech you
Make no more offers, use no farther means,
82 But with all brief and plain conveniency
Let me have judgment, and the Jew his will.

BASSANIO
For thy three thousand ducats here is six.

SHYLOCK
If every ducat in six thousand ducats
Were in six parts, and every part a ducat,
87 I would not draw them. I would have my bond.

DUKE
How shalt thou hope for mercy, rendering none?

SHYLOCK
What judgment shall I dread, doing no wrong?
90 You have among you many a purchased slave,
Which like your asses and your dogs and mules
92 You use in abject and in slavish parts,
Because you bought them. Shall I say to you,
"Let them be free! Marry them to your heirs!
Why sweat they under burdens? Let their beds

---

70 *think* keep in mind; *question* argue   72 *main flood* sea at flood tide; *bate* reduce   76 *wag* sway, bend   77 *fretten* fretted, vexed   82 *conveniency* propriety   87 *draw* take   92 *parts* duties, functions

Be made as soft as yours, and let their palates
Be seasoned with such viands"? You will answer,
"The slaves are ours." So do I answer you.
The pound of flesh which I demand of him
Is dearly bought, 'tis mine, and I will have it.   100
If you deny me, fie upon your law!
There is no force in the decrees of Venice.
I stand for judgment. Answer: shall I have it?

DUKE
Upon my power I may dismiss this court   104
Unless Bellario, a learned doctor
Whom I have sent for to determine this,   106
Come here today.   107

SALERIO   My lord, here stays without
A messenger with letters from the doctor,
New come from Padua.

DUKE
Bring us the letters. Call the messenger.   110

BASSANIO
Good cheer, Antonio! What, man, courage yet!
The Jew shall have my flesh, blood, bones, and all,
Ere thou shalt lose for me one drop of blood.

ANTONIO
I am a tainted wether of the flock,   114
Meetest for death; the weakest kind of fruit   115
Drops earliest to the ground, and so let me.
You cannot better be employed, Bassanio,
Than to live still, and write mine epitaph.

   Enter Nerissa [dressed as a lawyer's clerk].

DUKE
Came you from Padua, from Bellario?

NERISSA
From both, my lord. Bellario greets your grace.   120

---

104 *Upon* in accordance with   106 *determine this* resolve this issue   107
stays without waits outside   114 *wether* castrated ram   115 *Meetest for death*
most fit for slaughter

[Presents a letter.]

BASSANIO
  Why dost thou whet thy knife so earnestly?

SHYLOCK
  To cut the forfeiture from that bankrupt there.

GRATIANO
123 Not on thy sole, but on thy soul, harsh Jew,
  Thou mak'st thy knife keen; but no metal can –
125 No, not the hangman's ax – bear half the keenness
  Of thy sharp envy. Can no prayers pierce thee?

SHYLOCK
  No, none that thou hast wit enough to make.

GRATIANO
128 O be thou damned, inexecrable dog,
129 And for thy life let justice be accused!
130 Thou almost mak'st me waver in my faith,
131 To hold opinion with Pythagoras
  That souls of animals infuse themselves
  Into the trunks of men. Thy currish spirit
  Governed a wolf who, hanged for human slaughter,
135 Even from the gallows did his fell soul fleet,
136 And whilst thou layest in thy unhallowed dam
  Infused itself in thee; for thy desires
  Are wolvish, bloody, starved, and ravenous.

SHYLOCK
  Till thou canst rail the seal from off my bond,
140 Thou but offend'st thy lungs to speak so loud.
  Repair thy wit, good youth, or it will fall
  To cureless ruin. I stand here for law.

DUKE
  This letter from Bellario doth commend

---

123 *sole* (many productions have Shylock sharpen his knife on his shoe here)
125 *hangman's* executioner's 128 *inexecrable dog* dog that cannot be exe-
crated (cursed) enough 129 *for thy life* i.e., because you are allowed to live
131 *Pythagoras* Greek philosopher who thought souls migrated at death into
another living creature 135 *fell* cruel; *fleet* pass 136 *dam* mother (typically
a word applied to animals, not humans)

A young and learned doctor to our court.
Where is he?

NERISSA   He attendeth here hard by
To know your answer whether you'll admit him.

DUKE
With all my heart. Some three or four of you
Go give him courteous conduct to this place.
Meantime the court shall hear Bellario's letter.
    [Reads.]
"Your grace shall understand that at the receipt of your   150
letter I am very sick; but in the instant that your messenger came, in loving visitation was with me a young
doctor of Rome. His name is Balthasar. I acquainted
him with the cause in controversy between the Jew and
Antonio the merchant. We turned o'er many books together. He is furnished with my opinion which, bet-
tered with his own learning, the greatness whereof I
cannot enough commend, comes with him at my im-   158
portunity to fill up your grace's request in my stead. I
beseech you let his lack of years be no impediment to   160
let him lack a reverend estimation, for I never knew so
young a body with so old a head. I leave him to your
gracious acceptance, whose trial shall better publish his   163
commendation."
    Enter Portia [dressed as a doctor of laws] for
    Balthasar.
You hear the learn'd Bellario, what he writes;
And here, I take it, is the doctor come.
Give me your hand. Come you from old Bellario?

PORTIA
I did, my lord.

150–64 *"Your grace . . . commendation."* (no reader is designated in the early
texts, and it is possible that the letter is read by the duke or by Nerissa, the
"clerk") **158** *comes with him* i.e., brings my opinion **160–61** *to let him
lack* i.e., which will cause him to lack **163** *trial* i.e., actual performance

DUKE   You are welcome; take your place.
169   Are you acquainted with the difference
170   That holds this present question in the court?

PORTIA
171   I am informèd throughly of the cause.
172   Which is the merchant here and which the Jew?

DUKE
       Antonio and old Shylock, both stand forth.

PORTIA
       Is your name Shylock?

SHYLOCK   Shylock is my name.

PORTIA
       Of a strange nature is the suit you follow,
176   Yet in such rule that the Venetian law
177   Cannot impugn you as you do proceed.
           [To Antonio]
178   You stand within his danger, do you not?

ANTONIO
       Ay, so he says.

PORTIA   Do you confess the bond?

ANTONIO
180   I do.

PORTIA   Then must the Jew be merciful.

SHYLOCK
       On what compulsion must I? Tell me that.

PORTIA
182   The quality of mercy is not strained;
183   It droppeth as the gentle rain from heaven
       Upon the place beneath. It is twice blessed;
       It blesseth him that gives and him that takes.
       'Tis mightiest in the mightiest; it becomes

169–70 *with . . . court* i.e., with the case being tried   171 *throughly* thoroughly (the quarto's obsolete *throughly* is important rhythmically); *cause* case   172 *Which . . . Jew* (In performance a key moment – does Portia not distinguish Shylock from Antonio, or are they undistinguishable, or is she pretending she cannot distinguish plaintiff and defendant?)   176 *in such rule* so within the rules   177 *impugn* oppose, regard as illegal   178 *danger* power, control   182 *strained* constrained, forced   183 *rain* i.e., heavenly mercy (are Ecclesiasticus 35:20 and *Hamlet* III. 3.45)

The thronèd monarch better than his crown.
His scepter shows the force of temporal power,
The attribute to awe and majesty,
Wherein doth sit the dread and fear of kings;   190
But mercy is above this sceptered sway.
It is enthronèd in the hearts of kings,
It is an attribute to God himself,
And earthly power doth then show likest God's
When mercy seasons justice. Therefore, Jew,
Though justice be thy plea, consider this:
That in the course of justice none of us   197
Should see salvation. We do pray for mercy,
And that same prayer doth teach us all to render
The deeds of mercy. I have spoke thus much   200
To mitigate the justice of thy plea,   201
Which if thou follow, this strict court of Venice
Must needs give sentence 'gainst the merchant there.

SHYLOCK
My deeds upon my head! I crave the law,
The penalty and forfeit of my bond.

PORTIA
Is he not able to discharge the money?

BASSANIO
Yes, here I tender it for him in the court,
Yea, thrice the sum. If that will not suffice,
I will be bound to pay it ten times o'er
On forfeit of my hands, my head, my heart.   210
If this will not suffice, it must appear
That malice bears down truth. And I beseech you,   212
Wrest once the law to your authority: 213
To do a great right, do a little wrong,
And curb this cruel devil of his will.

PORTIA
It must not be. There is no power in Venice

---

197 *in . . . justice* i.e., if justice should actually run its course   **201** *mitigate*
temper, moderate; *the justice . . . plea* your appeal to strict justice   **212** *bears*
down overwhelms   **213** *Wrest . . . law* i.e., for once, subject the law

Can alter a decree establishèd.
'Twill be recorded for a precedent,
219   And many an error by the same example
220   Will rush into the state: it cannot be.

SHYLOCK
221   A Daniel come to judgment! Yea, a Daniel!
O wise young judge, how I do honor thee!

PORTIA
I pray you let me look upon the bond.

SHYLOCK
Here 'tis, most reverend doctor, here it is.

PORTIA
Shylock, there's thrice thy money offered thee.

SHYLOCK
An oath, an oath! I have an oath in heaven!
Shall I lay perjury upon my soul?
No, not for Venice!

PORTIA   Why, this bond is forfeit,
And lawfully by this the Jew may claim
230   A pound of flesh, to be by him cut off
Nearest the merchant's heart. Be merciful.
Take thrice thy money; bid me tear the bond.

SHYLOCK
233   When it is paid, according to the tenor.
It doth appear you are a worthy judge;
You know the law, your exposition
Hath been most sound. I charge you by the law,
Whereof you are a well-deserving pillar,
Proceed to judgment. By my soul I swear
There is no power in the tongue of man
240   To alter me. I stay here on my bond.

ANTONIO
Most heartily I do beseech the court

---

219 *error* exception to establish legal precedent   221 *Daniel* the shrewd
young man and judge who exposed the elders in their false charges against
Susannah (see the apocryphal Book of Susannah)   233 *tenor* substance of its
terms   240 *stay* stand

To give the judgment.
PORTIA   Why then, thus it is:
    You must prepare your bosom for his knife –
SHYLOCK
    O noble judge! O excellent young man!
PORTIA
    For the intent and purpose of the law
    Hath full relation to the penalty,   246
    Which here appeareth due upon the bond.
SHYLOCK
    'Tis very true. O wise and upright judge,
    How much more elder art thou than thy looks!
PORTIA
    Therefore lay bare your bosom.   250
SHYLOCK   Ay, his breast,
    So says the bond, doth it not, noble judge?
    "Nearest his heart": those are the very words.
PORTIA
    It is so. Are there balance here to weigh   253
    The flesh?
SHYLOCK   I have them ready.
PORTIA
    Have by some surgeon, Shylock, on your charge,   255
    To stop his wounds, lest he do bleed to death.
SHYLOCK
    Is it so nominated in the bond?
PORTIA
    It is not so expressed, but what of that?
    'Twere good you do so much for charity.
SHYLOCK
    I cannot find it; 'tis not in the bond.   260
PORTIA
    You, merchant, have you anything to say?
ANTONIO
    But little. I am armed and well prepared.

---

246 *Hath full relation to* is completely in accord with   **253** *balance* scales
255 *charge* expense

Give me your hand, Bassanio; fare you well.
Grieve not that I am fall'n to this for you,
For herein Fortune shows herself more kind
Than is her custom: it is still her use
To let the wretched man outlive his wealth
To view with hollow eye and wrinkled brow
An age of poverty; from which ling'ring penance
270   Of such misery doth she cut me off.
Commend me to your honorable wife.
272   Tell her the process of Antonio's end,
273   Say how I loved you, speak me fair in death,
And when the tale is told, bid her be judge
Whether Bassanio had not once a love.
276   Repent but you that you shall lose your friend,
And he repents not that he pays your debt;
For if the Jew do cut but deep enough,
I'll pay it instantly with all my heart.

BASSANIO
280   Antonio, I am married to a wife
Which is as dear to me as life itself;
But life itself, my wife, and all the world
Are not with me esteemed above thy life.
I would lose all, ay, sacrifice them all
Here to this devil, to deliver you.

PORTIA
Your wife would give you little thanks for that
If she were by to hear you make the offer.

GRATIANO
I have a wife who I protest I love.
I would she were in heaven, so she could
290   Entreat some power to change this currish Jew.

NERISSA
'Tis well you offer it behind her back;
The wish would make else an unquiet house.

---

272 *process* course (with pun on "legal proceeding"?) 273 *speak me fair*
speak well of me 276 *Repent . . . you* i.e., if only you regret (*repents* in the
next line also means "regrets")

SHYLOCK
  These be the Christian husbands! I have a daughter;
  Would any of the stock of Barabbas   294
  Had been her husband, rather than a Christian!
  We trifle time. I pray thee pursue sentence.
PORTIA
  A pound of that same merchant's flesh is thine.
  The court awards it, and the law doth give it –
SHYLOCK
  Most rightful judge!
PORTIA
  And you must cut this flesh from off his breast.   300
  The law allows it, and the court awards it.
SHYLOCK
  Most learnèd judge! A sentence: come, prepare!
PORTIA
  Tarry a little, there is something else.
  This bond doth give thee here no jot of blood;
  The words expressly are "a pound of flesh."
  Take then thy bond, take thou thy pound of flesh;
  But in the cutting it if thou dost shed
  One drop of Christian blood, thy lands and goods
  Are by the laws of Venice confiscate
  Unto the state of Venice.   310
GRATIANO
  O upright judge! Mark, Jew – O learnèd judge!
SHYLOCK
  Is that the law?
PORTIA   Thyself shalt see the act;
  For, as thou urgest justice, be assured
  Thou shalt have justice more than thou desirest.
GRATIANO
  O learnèd judge! Mark, Jew. A learnèd judge!

---

294 *Barabbas* a thief set free by Pontius Pilate when Jesus was condemned;
also the central character's name ("Barabas") in Christopher Marlowe's play
The Jew of Malta (Shylock prefers Jessica to have married a Jewish thief rather
than Lorenzo, a Christian thief)

SHYLOCK
  I take this offer then. Pay the bond thrice
  And let the Christian go.
BASSANIO   Here is the money.
PORTIA
318 Soft!
  The Jew shall have all justice. Soft, no haste;
320 He shall have nothing but the penalty.
GRATIANO
  O Jew! An upright judge, a learnèd judge!
PORTIA
  Therefore prepare thee to cut off the flesh.
  Shed thou no blood, nor cut thou less nor more
324 But just a pound of flesh. If thou tak'st more
  Or less than a just pound, be it but so much
326 As makes it light or heavy in the substance
  Or the division of the twentieth part
328 Of one poor scruple – nay, if the scale do turn
329 But in the estimation of a hair –
330 Thou diest, and all thy goods are confiscate.
GRATIANO
  A second Daniel; a Daniel, Jew!
332 Now, infidel, I have you on the hip!
PORTIA
  Why doth the Jew pause? Take thy forfeiture.
SHYLOCK
  Give me my principal, and let me go.
BASSANIO
  I have it ready for thee; here it is.
PORTIA
  He hath refused it in the open court.
  He shall have merely justice and his bond.

---

318 *Soft* wait **324** *just* exactly **326–27** *substance . . . division* quantity or a fraction **328** *scruple* one gram in apothecaries' weight (hence a very small amount) **329** *estimation of a hair* a hair's breadth **332** *on the hip* (cf. I.3.43)

GRATIANO
    A Daniel still say I, a second Daniel!
    I thank thee, Jew, for teaching me that word.

SHYLOCK
    Shall I not have barely my principal?   340

PORTIA
    Thou shalt have nothing but the forfeiture,
    To be so taken at thy peril, Jew.

SHYLOCK
    Why, then the devil give him good of it!
    I'll stay no longer question.   344

PORTIA   Tarry, Jew!
    The law hath yet another hold on you.
    It is enacted in the laws of Venice,
    If it be proved against an alien
    That by direct or indirect attempts
    He seek the life of any citizen,
    The party 'gainst the which he doth contrive   350
    Shall seize one half his goods; the other half
    Comes to the privy coffer of the state;   352
    And the offender's life lies in the mercy   353
    Of the duke only, 'gainst all other voice.
    In which predicament I say thou stand'st,
    For it appears by manifest proceeding
    That indirectly, and directly too,
    Thou hast contrived against the very life
    Of the defendant, and thou hast incurred
    The danger formerly by me rehearsed.   360
    Down therefore, and beg mercy of the duke.

GRATIANO
    Beg that thou mayst have leave to hang thyself!
    And yet, thy wealth being forfeit to the state,
    Thou hast not left the value of a cord;

---

340 *barely* even **344** *stay . . . question* press my case no further **352**
privy . . . state personal funds of the sovereign **353** *lies in* lies at **360** *danger . . . rehearsed* penalty I have cited

365 Therefore thou must be hanged at the state's charge.

DUKE
That thou shalt see the difference of our spirit,
I pardon thee thy life before thou ask it.
368 For half thy wealth, it is Antonio's;
The other half comes to the general state,
370 Which humbleness may drive unto a fine.

PORTIA
371 Ay, for the state, not for Antonio.

SHYLOCK
Nay, take my life and all! Pardon not that!
373 You take my house when you do take the prop
That doth sustain my house; you take my life
When you do take the means whereby I live.

PORTIA
What mercy can you render him, Antonio?

GRATIANO
377 A halter gratis, nothing else, for God's sake!

ANTONIO
So please my lord the duke and all the court
379 To quit the fine for one half of his goods,
380 I am content; so he will let me have
381 The other half in use, to render it
Upon his death unto the gentleman
That lately stole his daughter.
Two things provided more: that for this favor
385 He presently become a Christian;
The other, that he do record a gift
Here in the court of all he dies possessed
Unto his son Lorenzo and his daughter.

---

365 *charge* expense   368 *For* as for   370 *Which . . . fine* which humility on
your part may reduce to a fine   371 *Ay . . . Antonio* (Portia specifies that a
fine might replace the state's, not Antonio's, half of Shylock's fortune)   373
house (1) dwelling, (2) family, lineage   377 *halter* hangman's noose   379
quit remit (Antonio is proposing that Venice neither confiscate half of Shylock's wealth nor fine him)   381 *in use* in trust (but the earlier meaning,
"lend at interest," is probably present: see I.3.110)   385 *presently* immediately

DUKE
He shall do this, or else I do recant   389
The pardon that I late pronouncèd here.   390
PORTIA
Art thou contented, Jew? What dost thou say?   391
SHYLOCK
I am content.
PORTIA   Clerk, draw a deed of gift.
SHYLOCK
I pray you give me leave to go from hence;
I am not well. Send the deed after me,
And I will sign it.
DUKE   Get thee gone, but do it.
GRATIANO
In christening shalt thou have two godfathers.
Had I been judge, thou shouldst have had ten more – 397
To bring thee to the gallows, not to the font.
                              Exit [Shylock].

DUKE
Sir, I entreat you home with me to dinner.
PORTIA
I humbly do desire your grace of pardon.   400
I must away this night toward Padua,
And it is meet I presently set forth.
DUKE
I am sorry that your leisure serves you not.   403
Antonio, gratify this gentleman,   404
For in my mind you are much bound to him.
                        Exit Duke and his train.

BASSANIO
Most worthy gentleman, I and my friend
Have by your wisdom been this day acquitted
Of grievous penalties, in lieu whereof,   408

---

389 *recant* withdraw 391 *contented* i.e., willing to accept these terms 397
ten more i.e., to make a jury of twelve 403 *your leisure . . . not* i.e., you do
not have leisure 404 *gratify* reward 408 *in lieu whereof* in return for which

Three thousand ducats due unto the Jew
410   We freely cope your courteous pains withal.

ANTONIO
And stand indebted, over and above,
In love and service to you evermore.

PORTIA
He is well paid that is well satisfied,
And I delivering you am satisfied,
And therein do account myself well paid;
My mind was never yet more mercenary.
I pray you know me when we meet again.
I wish you well, and so I take my leave.

BASSANIO
419   Dear sir, of force I must attempt you further.
420   Take some remembrance of us as a tribute,
Not as fee. Grant me two things, I pray you –
Not to deny me, and to pardon me.

PORTIA
You press me far, and therefore I will yield.
Give me your gloves; I'll wear them for your sake.
And for your love I'll take this ring from you.
Do not draw back your hand; I'll take no more,
And you in love shall not deny me this.

BASSANIO
This ring, good sir, alas, it is a trifle!
I will not shame myself to give you this.

PORTIA
430   I will have nothing else but only this,
And now methinks I have a mind to it.

BASSANIO
432   There's more depends on this than on the value.
The dearest ring in Venice will I give you,
And find it out by proclamation.
435   Only for this, I pray you pardon me.

---

410 *cope* repay   419 *attempt you* try to persuade you   432 *There's . . . value*
more than the ring's value is involved in this   435 *for this* as for this ring;
pardon me i.e., release me from my obligation

PORTIA
    I see, sir, you are liberal in offers.
    You taught me first to beg, and now methinks
    You teach me how a beggar should be answered.

BASSANIO
    Good sir, this ring was given me by my wife,
    And when she put it on she made me vow   *440*
    That I should neither sell nor give nor lose it.

PORTIA
    That scuse serves many men to save their gifts.   *442*
    And if your wife be not a mad woman,
    And know how well I have deserved this ring,
    She would not hold out enemy for ever
    For giving it to me. Well, peace be with you.
                  Exeunt [Portia and Nerissa].

ANTONIO
    My Lord Bassanio, let him have the ring.
    Let his deservings, and my love withal,
    Be valued 'gainst your wife's commandement.   *449*

BASSANIO
    Go, Gratiano, run and overtake him;   *450*
    Give him the ring and bring him if thou canst
    Unto Antonio's house. Away, make haste.
                  Exit Gratiano.
    Come, you and I will thither presently,
    And in the morning early will we both
    Fly toward Belmont. Come, Antonio.   *Exeunt.*

                      *

∾ **IV.2** *Enter [Portia and] Nerissa [disguised as before].*

PORTIA
    Inquire the Jew's house out, give him this deed,   1
    And let him sign it. We'll away tonight
    And be a day before our husbands home.

---

442 *scuse* excuse   **449** *commandement* (pronounced as four syllables)
    IV.2 A street in Venice   **1** *deed* deed of gift (see V.1.292–93)

This deed will be well welcome to Lorenzo.
Enter Gratiano.

GRATIANO
5   Fair sir, you are well o'erta'en.
6   My Lord Bassanio upon more advice
    Hath sent you here this ring, and doth entreat
    Your company at dinner.

PORTIA   That cannot be.
    His ring I do accept most thankfully,
10 And so I pray you tell him. Furthermore,
    I pray you show my youth old Shylock's house.

GRATIANO
    That will I do.

NERISSA   Sir, I would speak with you.
    [Aside to Portia]
    I'll see if I can get my husband's ring,
    Which I did make him swear to keep for ever.

PORTIA   *[Aside to Nerissa]*
15 Thou mayst, I warrant. We shall have old swearing
    That they did give the rings away to men;
    But we'll outface them, and outswear them too. –
    Away, make haste! Thou know'st where I will tarry.

NERISSA
    Come, good sir, will you show me to this house?
                                            [Exeunt.]

                        *

∾ **V.1** *Enter Lorenzo and Jessica.*

LORENZO
    The moon shines bright. In such a night as this,
    When the sweet wind did gently kiss the trees
    And they did make no noise, in such a night

---

5 *o'erta'en* overtaken 6 *advice* consideration 15 *old* i.e., plenty of, con-
tinuous
    V.1 The grounds of Portia's house

Troilus methinks mounted the Troyan walls,   4
And sighed his soul toward the Grecian tents
Where Cressid lay that night.

JESSICA   In such a night
Did Thisby fearfully o'ertrip the dew,   7
And saw the lion's shadow ere himself,   8
And ran dismayed away.

LORENZO   In such a night
Stood Dido with a willow in her hand   10
Upon the wild sea banks, and waft her love   11
To come again to Carthage.

JESSICA   In such a night
Medea gathered the enchanted herbs   13
That did renew old Aeson.   14

LORENZO   In such a night
Did Jessica steal from the wealthy Jew   15
And with an unthrift love did run from Venice   16
As far as Belmont.

JESSICA   In such a night
Did young Lorenzo swear he loved her well,
Stealing her soul with many vows of faith,   19
And ne'er a true one.   20

LORENZO   In such a night
Did pretty Jessica, like a little shrew,
Slander her love, and he forgave it her.

JESSICA
I would outnight you, did nobody come:

4–14 *Troilus . . . Aeson* (these legendary stories of doomed lovers derive their
details from Ovid and Chaucer) 4 *Troilus* Trojan whose beloved, eventually
false, Cressida was sent unwillingly to the Greek camp 7 *Thisby* beloved of
Pyramus; she fled from the lovers' meeting place when a lion approached
8 *ere* before 10 *Dido* queen of Carthage loved, then deserted, by Aeneas;
willow willow branch (symbol of forsaken love) 11 *waft* beckoned 13
Medea enchantress in the legend of Jason and the Golden Fleece 14 *Aeson*
Jason's father 15 *steal* slip away (but the other meaning, "rob," is likely present) 16 *unthrift love* unthrifty love (?), unthrifty lover – i.e., Lorenzo (?)
19 *Stealing her soul* (Jessica may be joking playfully, but she has also converted to Christianity for Lorenzo's sake)

But hark, I hear the footing of a man.
Enter [Stephano,] a messenger.
LORENZO
Who comes so fast in silence of the night?
MESSENGER   A friend.
LORENZO
A friend? What friend? Your name I pray you, friend.
MESSENGER
Stephano is my name, and I bring word
My mistress will before the break of day
30   Be here at Belmont. She doth stray about
31   By holy crosses where she kneels and prays
For happy wedlock hours.
LORENZO   Who comes with her?
MESSENGER
None but a holy hermit and her maid.
I pray you, is my master yet returned?
LORENZO
He is not, nor we have not heard from him.
But go we in, I pray thee, Jessica,
And ceremoniously let us prepare
Some welcome for the mistress of the house.
Enter [Lancelot the] Clown.
39   LANCELOT   Sola, sola! Wo ha! Ho sola, sola!
40   LORENZO   Who calls?
LANCELOT   Sola! Did you see Master Lorenzo? Master
Lorenzo! Sola, sola!
LORENZO   Leave holloaing, man! Here.
LANCELOT   Sola! Where, where?
LORENZO   Here!
LANCELOT   Tell him there's a post come from my master,
with his horn full of good news. My master will be here
48   ere morning, sweet soul.   *[Exit.]*

---

31 *holy crosses* wayside shrines marked with crosses   39 *Sola* (sound imitat-
ing a post horn; see ll.46–47)   48 (Lancelot might exit here: he has no further dialogue)

LORENZO

    Let's in, and there expect their coming.

    And yet no matter: why should we go in?   *50*

    My friend Stephano, signify, I pray you,   *51*

    Within the house, your mistress is at hand,

    And bring your music forth into the air.

                             [Exit Stephano.]

    How sweet the moonlight sleeps upon this bank!

    Here will we sit and let the sounds of music

    Creep in our ears; soft stillness and the night

    Become the touches of sweet harmony.   *57*

    Sit, Jessica. Look how the floor of heaven

    Is thick inlaid with patens of bright gold.   *59*

    There's not the smallest orb which thou behold'st   *60*

    But in his motion like an angel sings,   *61*

    Still quiring to the young-eyed cherubins;   *62*

    Such harmony is in immortal souls,

    But whilst this muddy vesture of decay   *64*

    Doth grossly close it in, we cannot hear it.

      [Enter Musicians.]

    Come ho, and wake Diana with a hymn.   *66*

    With sweetest touches pierce your mistress' ear

    And draw her home with music.

      Play music.

JESSICA

    I am never merry when I hear sweet music.   *69*

LORENZO

    The reason is, your spirits are attentive.   *70*

    For do but note a wild and wanton herd

    Or race of youthful and unhandled colts   *72*

    Fetching mad bounds, bellowing and neighing loud,

    Which is the hot condition of their blood;

---

51 *signify* announce   **57** *Become* befit; *touches* notes, strains   **59** *patens* metal plates or tiling   **61** *motion . . . sings* (reference to the music of the spheres) **62** *quiring* choiring, singing   **64** *muddy vesture* clay (i.e., flesh)   **66** *Diana* the virgin moon goddess   **69** *merry* lighthearted   **72** *unhandled colts* unbroken young stallions

If they but hear perchance a trumpet sound,
Or any air of music touch their ears,
77   You shall perceive them make a mutual stand,
Their savage eyes turned to a modest gaze
79   By the sweet power of music. Therefore the poet
80   Did feign that Orpheus drew trees, stones, and floods;
81   Since nought so stockish, hard, and full of rage
But music for the time doth change his nature.
The man that hath no music in himself,
Nor is not moved with concord of sweet sounds,
85   Is fit for treasons, stratagems, and spoils;
The motions of his spirit are dull as night,
87   And his affections dark as Erebus.
Let no such man be trusted. Mark the music.
    Enter Portia and Nerissa.

PORTIA
That light we see is burning in my hall;
90   How far that little candle throws his beams!
91   So shines a good deed in a naughty world.

NERISSA
When the moon shone we did not see the candle.

PORTIA
So doth the greater glory dim the less.
94   A substitute shines brightly as a king
Until a king be by, and then his state
Empties itself, as doth an inland brook
Into the main of waters. Music, hark!

NERISSA
98   It is your music, madam, of the house.

PORTIA
99   Nothing is good, I see, without respect;
100   Methinks it sounds much sweeter than by day.

---

77 *make . . . stand* all stand still together   79 *poet* Ovid, in *Metamorphoses*,
10   80 *feign* imagine; *Orpheus* legendary musician; *drew* attracted, bent to
his musical spell   81 *stockish* blockish, dull   85 *spoils* plundering   87 *Erebus* classical place of darkness in the region of hell   91 *naughty* wicked (see
Matthew 5:14–16)   94 *substitute* deputy (of the king)   98 *music* group of
musicians   99 *without respect* without reference to accompanying things

NERISSA

   Silence bestows that virtue on it, madam.

PORTIA

   The crow doth sing as sweetly as the lark

   When neither is attended; and I think   103

   The nightingale, if she should sing by day

   When every goose is cackling, would be thought

   No better a musician than the wren.

   How many things by season seasoned are   107

   To their right praise and true perfection.

   Peace! How the moon sleeps with Endymion,   109

   And would not be awaked.   *110*

      [Music ceases.]

LORENZO   That is the voice,

   Or I am much deceived, of Portia.

PORTIA

   He knows me as the blind man knows the cuckoo –

   By the bad voice.

LORENZO   Dear lady, welcome home.

PORTIA

   We have been praying for our husbands' welfare,

   Which speed we hope the better for our words.   115

   Are they returned?

LORENZO   Madam, they are not yet,

   But there is come a messenger before

   To signify their coming.

PORTIA   Go in, Nerissa.

   Give order to my servants that they take

   No note at all of our being absent hence –   *120*

   Nor you, Lorenzo, Jessica nor you.   *121*

      [A tucket sounds.]

LORENZO

   Your husband is at hand; I hear his trumpet.

---

103 *attended* noticed (?), expected (?)   **107–8** *by season . . . perfection* i.e., are
made perfect by coming at the right time   **109** *Endymion* shepherd loved by
the moon goddess (the line is apparently an elaborate way of saying the
moon has passed behind a cloud: see l. 92)   **115** *speed* prosper   **121** s.d.
tucket short flourish of trumpets

We are no telltales, madam; fear you not.

PORTIA

This night methinks is but the daylight sick;
It looks a little paler. 'Tis a day
Such as the day is when the sun is hid.

Enter Bassanio, Antonio, Gratiano, and their
followers.

BASSANIO

127   We should hold day with the antipodes
If you would walk in absence of the sun.

PORTIA

129   Let me give light, but let me not be light,
130   For a light wife doth make a heavy husband,
And never be Bassanio so for me.

132   But God sort all! You are welcome home, my lord.

BASSANIO

I thank you, madam. Give welcome to my friend.
This is the man, this is Antonio,
To whom I am so infinitely bound.

PORTIA

136   You should in all sense be much bound to him,
For, as I hear, he was much bound for you.

ANTONIO

138   No more than I am well acquitted of.

PORTIA

Sir, you are very welcome to our house.
140   It must appear in other ways than words:
141   Therefore I scant this breathing courtesy.

GRATIANO   *[To Nerissa]*

By yonder moon I swear you do me wrong!
In faith, I gave it to the judge's clerk.
144   Would he were gelt that had it, for my part,

---

127 *hold . . . antipodes* i.e., share daylight with the other side of the earth
129 *be light* i.e., be unfaithful   130 *heavy* sad   132 *sort* dispose   136 *in all*
sense in every meaning of the word   138 *acquitted of* released from   141
scant . . . courtesy cut short this courtesy of breath – i.e., of words   144 *gelt*
gelded; *for my part* so far as I am concerned

Since you do take it, love, so much at heart.

PORTIA
A quarrel ho, already! What's the matter?

GRATIANO
About a hoop of gold, a paltry ring
That she did give me, whose posy was   148
For all the world like cutler's poetry   149
Upon a knife – "Love me, and leave me not."   *150*

NERISSA
What talk you of the posy or the value?   151
You swore to me when I did give it you
That you would wear it till your hour of death,
And that it should lie with you in your grave.
Though not for me, yet for your vehement oaths,   155
You should have been respective and have kept it.   156
Gave it a judge's clerk! No, God's my judge,
The clerk will ne'er wear hair on's face that had it!

GRATIANO
He will, an if he live to be a man.   159

NERISSA
Ay, if a woman live to be a man.   *160*

GRATIANO
Now by this hand, I gave it to a youth,
A kind of boy, a little scrubbèd boy   162
No higher than thyself, the judge's clerk,
A prating boy that begged it as a fee.
I could not for my heart deny it him.

PORTIA
You were to blame – I must be plain with you –
To part so slightly with your wife's first gift,
A thing stuck on with oaths upon your finger
And so riveted with faith unto your flesh.

---

148 *posy* inscription (commonly in verse)   **149** *cutler's poetry* banal verse or
stale mottoes carved in a knife handle   **151** *What* why   **155** *Though . . . yet
for* even if not for my sake, still because of   **156** *respective* concerned (for the
way you received it)   **159** *an if* if   **162** *scrubbèd* scrubby, short

170   I gave my love a ring, and made him swear
      Never to part with it, and here he stands.
172   I dare be sworn for him he would not leave it
      Nor pluck it from his finger for the wealth
      That the world masters. Now in faith, Gratiano,
      You give your wife too unkind a cause of grief.
176   An 'twere to me, I should be mad at it.

BASSANIO   *[Aside]*
      Why, I were best to cut my left hand off
      And swear I lost the ring defending it.

GRATIANO
      My Lord Bassanio gave his ring away
180   Unto the judge that begged it, and indeed
      Deserved it too; and then the boy his clerk
      That took some pains in writing, he begged mine;
      And neither man nor master would take aught
      But the two rings.

PORTIA   What ring gave you, my lord?
      Not that, I hope, which you received of me.

BASSANIO
186   If I could add a lie unto a fault,
      I would deny it; but you see my finger
      Hath not the ring upon it – it is gone.

PORTIA
      Even so void is your false heart of truth.
190   By heaven, I will ne'er come in your bed
      Until I see the ring!

NERISSA   Nor I in yours
      Till I again see mine!

BASSANIO   Sweet Portia,
      If you did know to whom I gave the ring,
      If you did know for whom I gave the ring,
      And would conceive for what I gave the ring,
      And how unwillingly I left the ring
      When nought would be accepted but the ring,
      You would abate the strength of your displeasure.

---

172 *leave* part with   176 *mad* (1) furious, (2) distracted   186 *fault* misdeed

PORTIA

    If you had known the virtue of the ring,   199

    Or half her worthiness that gave the ring,   *200*

    Or your own honor to contain the ring,   201

    You would not then have parted with the ring.

    What man is there so much unreasonable,

    If you had pleased to have defended it   204

    With any terms of zeal, wanted the modesty

    To urge the thing held as a ceremony?   206

    Nerissa teaches me what to believe:

    I'll die for't but some woman had the ring!   208

BASSANIO

    No, by my honor, madam! By my soul

    No woman had it, but a civil doctor,   210

    Which did refuse three thousand ducats of me

    And begged the ring, the which I did deny him,

    And suffered him to go displeased away –   213

    Even he that had held up the very life

    Of my dear friend. What should I say, sweet lady?

    I was enforced to send it after him.

    I was beset with shame and courtesy.   217

    My honor would not let ingratitude

    So much besmear it. Pardon me, good lady!

    For by these blessèd candles of the night,   *220*

    Had you been there I think you would have begged

    The ring of me to give the worthy doctor.

PORTIA

    Let not that doctor e'er come near my house.

    Since he hath got the jewel that I loved

    And that which you did swear to keep for me,

    I will become as liberal as you;

    I'll not deny him anything I have,

    No, not my body nor my husband's bed.

---

199 *virtue* power **201** *honor to contain* solemn duty to keep **204** *defended it* i.e., resisted giving it away **206** *urge* demand as a gift; *ceremony* token, keepsake **208** *but . . . had* if some woman didn't get **210** *civil doctor* doctor of civil law **213** *suffered* allowed **217** *beset with* attacked (or surrounded by)

229 Know him I shall, I am well sure of it.

230 Lie not a night from home; watch me like Argus.
　　 If you do not, if I be left alone,
　　 Now by mine honor which is yet mine own,
　　 I'll have that doctor for my bedfellow.

NERISSA

234 And I his clerk. Therefore be well advised
　　 How you do leave me to mine own protection.

GRATIANO

236 Well, do you so. Let not me take him then,

237 For if I do, I'll mar the young clerk's pen.

ANTONIO

　　 I am th' unhappy subject of these quarrels.

PORTIA

　　 Sir, grieve not you; you are welcome notwithstanding.

BASSANIO

240 Portia, forgive me this enforcèd wrong,
　　 And in the hearing of these many friends
　　 I swear to thee, even by thine own fair eyes,
　　 Wherein I see myself –

PORTIA　　　　　　　　Mark you but that!
　　 In both my eyes he doubly sees himself,

245 In each eye one. Swear by your double self,

246 And there's an oath of credit.

BASSANIO　　　　　　　　Nay, but hear me.
　　 Pardon this fault, and by my soul I swear .
　　 I never more will break an oath with thee.

ANTONIO

　　 I once did lend my body for his wealth,

250 Which but for him that had your husband's ring
　　 Had quite miscarried. I dare be bound again,
　　 My soul upon the forfeit, that your lord

---

229 *Know* (1) recognize, (2) have sexual intercourse with (see IV.1.417)
230 *Argus* mythological figure with a hundred eyes　**234** *well advised* very
careful　**236** *take* catch　**237** *pen* i.e., penis　**240** *enforcèd* unavoidable
245 *double* (1) twofold, (2) deceitful　**246** *oath of credit* oath that can be believed (said ironically)

Will never more break faith advisedly.   253

PORTIA
Then you shall be his surety. Give him this,
And bid him keep it better than the other.

ANTONIO
Here, Lord Bassanio. Swear to keep this ring.

BASSANIO
By heaven, it is the same I gave the doctor!

PORTIA
I had it of him. Pardon me, Bassanio,   258
For by this ring the doctor lay with me.

NERISSA
And pardon me, my gentle Gratiano,   *260*
For that same scrubbèd boy, the doctor's clerk,
In lieu of this last night did lie with me.   262

GRATIANO
Why, this is like the mending of highways
In summer, where the ways are fair enough.
What, are we cuckolds ere we have deserved it?   265

PORTIA
Speak not so grossly. You are all amazed.   266
Here is a letter; read it at your leisure.
It comes from Padua from Bellario.
There you shall find that Portia was the doctor,
Nerissa there her clerk. Lorenzo here   *270*
Shall witness I set forth as soon as you,
And even but now returned; I have not yet
Entered my house. Antonio, you are welcome,
And I have better news in store for you
Than you expect. Unseal this letter soon;
There you shall find three of your argosies
Are richly come to harbor suddenly.
You shall not know by what strange accident

---

253 *advisedly* intentionally   **258** *of him* from him   **262** *In lieu of* in return for   **265** *cuckolds* deceived husbands   **266** *amazed* lost in a maze, befuddled

279   I chancèd on this letter.
ANTONIO   I am dumb.
BASSANIO
280   Were you the doctor, and I knew you not?
GRATIANO
      Were you the clerk that is to make me cuckold?
NERISSA
      Ay, but the clerk that never means to do it,
      Unless he live until he be a man.
BASSANIO
      Sweet doctor, you shall be my bedfellow.
      When I am absent, then lie with my wife.
ANTONIO
286   Sweet lady, you have given me life and living,
      For here I read for certain that my ships
288   Are safely come to road.
PORTIA   How now, Lorenzo?
      My clerk hath some good comforts too for you.
NERISSA
290   Ay, and I'll give them him without a fee.
      There do I give to you and Jessica
      From the rich Jew, a special deed of gift,
      After his death, of all he dies possessed of.
LORENZO
294   Fair ladies, you drop manna in the way
      Of starvèd people.
PORTIA   It is almost morning,
296   And yet I am sure you are not satisfied
      Of these events at full. Let us go in,
298   And charge us there upon inter'gatories,
      And we will answer all things faithfully.
GRATIANO
300   Let it be so. The first inter'gatory

---

279 *dumb* silenced   286 *living* material means to live   288 *road* anchorage
294 *manna* i.e., food from heaven (see Exodus 16:15)   296–97 *satisfied . . .
full* fully satisfied with the explanation of these events   298 *charge . . . inter'gatories* require ourselves there to answer interrogatories (legally framed
questions answerable under oath)

That my Nerissa shall be sworn on is,
Whether till the next night she had rather stay,   302
Or go to bed now, being two hours to day.
But were the day come, I should wish it dark
Till I were couching with the doctor's clerk.   305
Well, while I live I'll fear no other thing
So sore as keeping safe Nerissa's ring.   *Exeunt.*   307

---

302 *stay* wait **305** *clerk* (pronounced "clark") **307** *ring* (with the bawdy meaning "vulva")

FOR THE BEST IN PAPERBACKS, LOOK FOR THE

The distinguished Pelican Shakespeare series, newly revised
to be the premier choice for students, professors, and
general readers well into the 21st century

All's Well That Ends Well
ISBN 0-14-071460-X

Antony and Cleopatra
ISBN 0-14-071452-9

As You Like It
ISBN 0-14-071471-5

The Comedy of Errors
ISBN 0-14-071474-X

Coriolanus
ISBN 0-14-071473-1

Cymbeline
ISBN 0-14-071472-3

Hamlet
ISBN 0-14-071454-5

Henry IV, Part I
ISBN 0-14-071456-1

Henry IV, Part 2
ISBN 0-14-071457-X

Henry V
ISBN 0-14-071458-8

Henry VI, Part 1
ISBN 0-14-071465-0

Henry VI, Part 2
ISBN 0-14-071466-9

Henry VI, Part 3
ISBN 0-14-071467-7

Henry VIII
ISBN 0-14-071475-8

Julius Caesar
ISBN 0-14-071468-5

King John
ISBN 0-14-071459-6

King Lear
ISBN 0-14-071476-6

King Lear
(The Quarto and Folio Texts)
ISBN 0-14-071490-1

Love's Labor's Lost
ISBN 0-14-071477-4

Macbeth
ISBN 0-14-071478-2

Measure for Measure
ISBN 0-14-071479-0

Romeo and Juliet
ISBN 0-14-071484-7

The Merchant of Venice
ISBN 0-14-071462-6

The Sonnets
ISBN 0-14-071453-7

The Merry Wives of Windsor
ISBN 0-14-071464-2

The Taming of the Shrew
ISBN 0-14-071451-0

A Midsummer Night's Dream
ISBN 0-14-071455-3

The Tempest
ISBN 0-14-071485-5

Much Ado About Nothing
ISBN 0-14-071480-4

Timon of Athens
ISBN 0-14-071487-1

The Narrative Poems
ISBN 0-14-071481-2

Titus Andronicus
ISBN 0-14-071491-X

Othello
ISBN 0-14-071463-4

Troilus and Cressida
ISBN 0-14-071486-3

Pericles
ISBN 0-14-071469-3

Twelfth Night
ISBN 0-14-071489-8

Richard II
ISBN 0-14-071482-0

The Two Gentlemen of Verona
ISBN 0-14-071461-8

Richard III
ISBN 0-14-071483-9

The Winter's Tale
ISBN 0-14-071488-X